Yet... I Will Rejoice

PALMETTO
PUBLISHING
Charleston, SC
www.PalmettoPublishing.com

Copyright © 2024 by Donna Carole Kitchens

Photo taken by Jeannie Earle in the Nantahala National Forest.

All rights reserved

No portion of this book may be reproduced, stored in a retrieval system, or transmitted in any form by any means–electronic, mechanical, photocopy, recording, or other–except for brief quotations in printed reviews, without prior permission of the author.

Unless otherwise indicated, scripture quotations are from the ESV® Bible (The Holy Bible, English Standard Version®), © 2001 by Crossway, a publishing ministry of Good News Publishers. Used by permission. All rights reserved. The ESV text may not be quoted in any publication made available to the public by a Creative Commons license. The ESV may not be translated in whole or in part into any other language.
(NIV-New International Version)
Scripture quotations marked NLT are taken from the *Holy Bible*, New Living Translation, Copyright © 1996, 2004, 2015 by Tyndale House Foundation. Used by permission of Tyndale House Publishers, Inc., Carol Stream, Illinois 60188. All rights reserved.

Paperback ISBN: 979-8-8229-5880-7

Yet... I Will Rejoice

TRUSTING THAT GOD IS STILL GOOD
WHILE LIVING WITH A DEVASTATING
CANCER DIAGNOSIS

DONNA CAROLE KITCHENS

*For my children and my grandchildren,
who daily give me a reason to fight.*

*For my Mommy, who demonstrates for me
what living daily for Christ and loving
family well looks like.*

*For my Daddy in heaven who lived
out unconditional love.*

*I love all of you, unconditionally,
every single day of my life.*

*To my precious Dr. B…thank you
for fighting as hard for me
as I fight for myself.*

I love you.

*Most of all, thank you to my Savior, Jesus,
for Your mercy and grace, Your unshakable love,
and this promise from Your Word that continually
sustains me: "The Lord will fight for you; you need
only to be still." (NIV)*

Contents

I Have Cancer 1

My Cancer Facts and FAQs (at the Time of Diagnosis) ... 10

I'm Fine 14

Fear and Faith 25

Tears upon Tears 33

Questions with No Answers 47

Change 62

Control 75

Exile 85

Not the End 96

I Have Cancer

> Though the fig tree should not blossom, nor fruit be on the vines, the produce of the olive fail and the fields yield no food, the flock be cut off from the fold and there be no herd in the stalls, yet I will rejoice in the Lord; I will take joy in the God of my salvation.
>
> Habakkuk 3:17–18

Sunday, February 11, 2018. A date that will be forever burned on my brain. I suspect that most people who have been diagnosed with cancer remember the date and the moment they first heard the words "You have cancer." And I am no exception. I had gone to the emergency room with a terrible pain in my right side. It had bothered me off and on for about a month, but since, according to the internet, my symptoms suggested that I had a gallstone, and since the pain came and went, I had chosen to ignore it. I had even said to coworkers that I didn't have time for a gallstone. But that day, the pain was worse than it had been, and I decided it was time to get it checked out. The ER doctor and the nurse I had both agreed that it sounded like a gall stone and the doctor ordered a CT scan to confirm. As I waited for the results, I remember thinking what horrible timing it was that I was likely going to have to have surgery. I had just returned from a week of training for a new job and taking time off to recover from surgery was definitely not on my agenda. Little did I know that the results of that CT would make those thoughts irrelevant. The doctor and nurse returned to the room, both looking very sullen. The doctor sat down and began talking. I don't remember much of what he said. Just that my gallbladder was fine, but that I had cancer. And he began listing everywhere the cancer had already spread. I remember becoming aware that I wasn't actually hearing what he was saying anymore. And I had to stop him and ask him to tell me again where all I had cancer. As he began the list again, I completely lost control. I only remember bits and pieces after that. I remember screaming for my mom. I remember someone handing me a cell phone with my mom on the line, though I have no idea what I said to her other than telling her I had cancer and then hearing my almost fifty-one-year-old self screaming into the phone, "MOMMY! I want my Mommy!" over and over. I remember the doctor giving instructions for the nurse to give me something to calm me down. I remember him saying they were sending me to an oncologist. And then I remember the overwhelming thought "RUN!" I think I tried to rip the IV out of my arm. I wasn't successful, but I don't remember the nurse taking it out for me. I don't remember leaving the hospital. I don't remember how I got home. I don't remember going into my house or going upstairs or getting into my bed. I don't remember making several phone calls or sending a few emails. I don't think it occurred to me to ask my daughter, who had been with me at the hospital, if she was OK. I don't know who told my boys what had just happened. I don't remember anything else about the remainder of that day. Nothing. And I remember very little about the next several days. But what I do remember can only be described as me being dragged through hell.

My first visit with an oncologist was incredibly encouraging. He looked at the CT from the hospital and said that what he was seeing did not look like cancer to him. He scheduled me for some exploratory surgery and biopsies two days later. Valentine's Day. After surgery, he met with my family in the waiting room and told them that he did see something of concern in my liver, and he took biopsies to determine what it was. But other than that, he wasn't "seeing that nasty cancer" I was told I had at the hospital. He said he would likely call before the end of the week with results from the biopsies. That call didn't come. By Tuesday of the next week, I was so anxious I couldn't wait any longer. I called and left a message at his office, and he called me back after office hours. It wasn't good news. The biopsies revealed that I did, in fact, have cancer. However, although my liver was heavily affected, it was not the primary source of my cancer. But they had not yet been able to determine what kind of cancer it was; therefore, they didn't know where it originated. He said they were continuing to run tests and he would call when they knew more. I did get a call on Friday, but just to be told they still had no answers. I asked if they had been able to rule anything out and was told they knew it wasn't lung cancer and it wasn't breast cancer. But because they were at the end of their testing abilities, they were sending my biopsies to Minnesota (Mayo Clinic). Again, waiting. And the call came the next Tuesday. "Mrs. Kitchens, you have breast cancer." By this time, the oncologist had already ordered a PET scan and had told me that because he was a gynecological oncologist and my cancer was not gynecological in nature, he would be referring me to a different oncologist. In hindsight, that referral is the singular thing that I am thankful for from him.

March 9, 2018. Almost a full month since first hearing the words "you have cancer," I meet my new oncologist. Immediately I know I am where I am supposed to be. The care he showed not just me, but each member of my family that was with me that day, was unbelievably compassionate. Although he was straightforward with giving me the news, the tenderness with which he delivered it was nothing short of precious. That was the day that I got the results of the PET scan. That was the day I saw my cancer literally glowing on a computer screen. That was the day that I was told it was stage IV. That was the day I first heard the words "treatable but not curable." That was the day that life as I knew it officially ended, and my life of cancer began. Yes, it had been almost a month since my initial diagnosis. Yes, I already knew that I had cancer. Yes, I knew I was going to begin treatment and that difficult days were ahead. But up until that day, it had all seemed like it was a different me that this was all happening to. Somehow it didn't become real until that day. Treatable but not curable. Those words cut through the fog that had shrouded everything that had happened in the last month. Those words made it all real. Those words shook me to the core of my being. Those words changed my future. My hopes and dreams. My everything. Those words ended my life before cancer and started my life with cancer. This was my life now. I have treatable but not curable cancer. I have cancer.

Cancer had become the focal point of my whole life. I was getting so much information that it took basically all of my energy to process it all. There wasn't room for much else. I learned that my official diagnosis was stage iv metastatic breast cancer (MBC). I learned that the type of breast cancer I have is HER2+, which means my cancer is fed by HER2 protein, not hormones. I learned what my immediate treatment plan was and, assuming the initial treatments worked as expected, what my long-term treatment plan was. I learned that "long-term treatment plan" meant that I would have treatments for the rest of my life. I learned that even if the initial treatments worked as expected, the nature of this type of cancer is to mutate and come back in a form that is resistant to the meds currently being used to control it, and that, assuming the original cancer was still responding well to the current meds, the mutation would be treated as a different cancer and would have its own treatment plan. I learned that in addition to my long-term treatments, I would have a regular schedule for scans to watch for renewed growth of the original cancer and for indications that it had spread to new places in my body. And I learned exactly where all I already had cancer. I was a couple of months into treatment before I looked at the list of where my cancer was located. Up until that point, I had been too overwhelmed, too emotionally fragile to handle that information. But when the time came that my oncologist and I thought I could finally handle it, it was still so shocking that it was truly a huge emotional setback for me. There's a lot of cancer. It's a lot to process.

For a while I was so overwhelmed that the words "I have cancer" seemed to precede every other thought I had. I have cancer, and I'm hungry. I have cancer, and I'm going to take a shower. I have cancer, and I need to go to the grocery store. Everything I thought or did felt secondary to the overwhelming knowledge that I had cancer. It took quite a while for me to get to the point where having cancer wasn't the predominant focal point of my world. It's been a slow process. To be honest, even now, there is some point in every day that I think about cancer. And to be even more honest, at some point every day I wonder if today is the day that my cancer comes back. I've just come to the place where I've accepted that cancer will always be a part of my life. Thinking about cancer will always be a part of my life. But I also reached a point where I had to decide if I was going to continue to let the fear and the "hard" of cancer control me. There is very little about cancer that is within my control. Cancer is a whole lifestyle for me now, and there is very little that I do in my life that I don't have to take cancer into consideration before taking a step. I have treatment every three weeks. I have a CT scan, a nuclear bone scan, and an echocardiogram every three months. I have an MRI of my brain every six months. These are not optional. These are the realities of living with cancer. I have to schedule everything else in my life around these things. That is just fact. And it would be easy to let these facts frustrate and overwhelm me and keep me in bondage to angriness and bitterness. But who wants to live like that? Certainly not me! So I had a decision to make. Do I want to focus on the control cancer has over my life, or do I want to try to do something positive with it all? And the answer was pretty easy. I decided I wanted to do something positive.

I had already started a Facebook page at that point. Initially, I had used it to keep my family and friends informed about what was going on. It was just easier to put all the details and updates in one place rather than having to make multiple phone call, send multiple emails and texts, etc. So since I already had that in place, I decided to use that as a format to get super honest, super transparent about what life with cancer is really like. And even more importantly, I wanted to get super honest about what it's like to try to learn to live with cancer as a Christian. I wanted to share how I was learning to cope with all the hard, and scary, and infuriating moments while still not just believing in God, but still believing that He is a good and loving and caring God. I wanted to share how I was learning to cope with everything that comes with a cancer diagnosis, treatments, scans, doctor visits, and the everyday, all-day battle with cancer, yet still finding ways to praise God and ways to have joy in spite of living with cancer. I decided that I wanted to try to use my experience, my journey with cancer to help someone else with theirs. I have been so blessed by what has come from that Facebook page and the decision to get brutally honest about my own experience. It has been hugely cathartic for me, and hopefully, it has given a little help to others along the way. So this book is my feeble attempt at taking my desire to share my journey in the hopes of helping others with theirs to a different format. My prayer is that you find something in this book that helps. Whether you're reading because you yourself are battling cancer, or you are walking alongside someone you love who is battling cancer, or even if you are battling something completely different, I pray that you will find something of encouragement here. And I pray that perhaps, even in the midst of your struggle, you, like me, will find that you can still rejoice.

My Cancer Facts and FAQs (at the Time of Diagnosis)

- Type of cancer: HER2+ metastatic breast cancer
- What stage: IV
- Where my cancer is located:
  - Right breast—large tumor
  - lymph node under right arm
  - liver—large tumor—and twenty-plus other spots
  - lymph node near liver, sternum—twenty-plus spots
  - spine—T8, T9, T10, T11, L3 (which eventually developed a fracture, causing it to collapse and have to be surgically repaired), L4
  - left humerus head
  - left seventh rib
  - left media
  - iliac bone

- o left femur head
- o left femur shaft
- Initial treatment plan: six chemotherapy and two antibody cancer drugs given in three-weeks intervals, drug to increase white blood cell count the day after each treatment, and bone-strengthening drug every six weeks
- Ongoing treatment plan:
  - o two antibody drugs given in three-week intervals and bone-strengthening drug every six months
  - o CT scan (neck to pelvic), echocardiogram, and nuclear bone scan (head to toe) every three months, brain MRI every six months
- What is HER2+ breast cancer? All the cells in the body, healthy and cancerous, haveHER2 receptors. But HER2+ breast cancer cells have too many HER2 receptors, which makes them grow and divide faster than other types of cells. This causes tumors to form.
- What is metastatic breast cancer? The word "metastatic" means cancer that has spread to other parts of the body.
- Where is HER2+ cancer most likely to spread to? Metastatic breast cancer is most likely to spread to bones, liver, lungs, and brain, but could also spread elsewhere in the body.
- Is HER2+ breast cancer aggressive? Yes, HER2+ positive breast cancers do tend to be more aggressive than other types of breast cancer

- Did I have a mastectomy? No. The purpose of a mastectomy is to prevent the cancer from spreading from the breast to other parts of the body. Because my cancer had already spread by the time I was diagnosed, a mastectomy would have introduced risks associated with a major surgery yet change nothing about my prognosis. So it was decided that the surgery was an unnecessary risk.
- What is the current status of my cancer? My cancer is currently stable, meaning it is neither growing nor shrinking.
- What is my prognosis? That is a question without a straightforward answer. But here are some of the things we know:
    o The meds I am on are working extremely well. I have been stable with no reoccurrences for longer than most patients with a similar diagnosis. However, my doctor compares it to a sleeping bear in a cave: just because you can't see it, it doesn't mean it's not there and that it won't wake up.
    o This is a smart and aggressive cancer. There is a great possibility that at some point my cancer will mutate and come back in a form that is resistant to the meds that I am currently on. If that happens, as long as my current cancer is still stable, I will remain on my current treatment meds, and the new cancer would have its own treatment regimen.

- Should the meds that I am currently on stop controlling my cancer, there are several other drugs already on the market that we could go to, and new drugs are always being developed. This gives me great hope.

I'm Fine

> O Lord, you have searched me and known me! You know when I sit down and when I rise up; you discern my thoughts from afar...Even before a word is on my tongue, behold, O Lord, you know it altogether.
>
> Psalm 139:1, 2, 4

One of the first things I did when I was diagnosed with cancer was call a friend who had battled breast cancer. There are many things I don't remember about that conversation, as it was either the day I was diagnosed or the day right after. I'm honestly not sure. But there are two things that I remember her telling me that I have carried with me to this day and that I have shared with others many times. The first was "stay off the internet." Although I do tend to consult the internet often about many things, cancer is rarely one of them. There is so much information out there that is conflicting or out of date. Much of it is personal opinion and not based on medical research. Some of it is straight medical research that it's hard to understand unless you have a medical degree. It can quickly become confusing and frustrating and extremely overwhelming. And, even more importantly, it can be extremely discouraging. Just recently I was looking for something very specific about my kind of cancer and got so much conflicting information I went back and forth between being encouraged by one article just to be discouraged by the next. So I try to stay away from most of it. The only time I really look up information about my cancer is when I've gotten a scan report that has a term in it that I am unfamiliar with. Then I will look up just that term and leave the rest to discussions with my doctor. I strongly encourage others to do the same. Your doctor knows you and your cancer better than any internet article ever will. So I suggest you take your questions there and not to your computer.

The other thing that my friend said to me that has really had an impact on me is that she would be there to answer any question I had about her experience—but that there would be times that she wouldn't be able to answer my questions. She explained that so much about cancer is extremely individualized. So much so that two people can have an almost identical diagnosis and an identical treatment plan and still have a completely different cancer experience. I have found that to be 100 percent true! I have met people over the last few years that also have HER2+ metastatic breast cancer and have had the same meds that I am on, but their cancer has not responded as well as mine has, or hasn't responded to them at all. I've met some that had horrible side effects to chemotherapy and some that had hardly any at all. I, myself, fell somewhere in-between with my side effects. One of my treatment meds can cause serious heart issues in many patients. I haven't shown any signs of heart problems, and I've been on this med for over five years now. There are very few absolutes about cancer and cancer treatment, and I try to be very careful in my discussions with other people about it for that very reason.

However, it has been my personal experience that there are a few things that are pretty much universal, but they don't really have anything to do with the medical side of life with cancer. They fall more into the category of social interactions about cancer. It's about the things people say to us or ask us about cancer. It's the way we feel we must respond in the face of those conversations. Almost every person I have talked to about this has had similar experiences and has felt compelled to respond in similar ways. Here are some examples:

Advice—For some reason, many people feel compelled to give a cancer patient a list of dos and don'ts now that they have cancer. Don't eat sugar. Change all your cleaning products to plants-based products. Throw away all of your makeup and skin care products and get "healthier" versions. Exercise a lot. Don't exercise too much. Go to a vegetarian diet. Don't get your nails done. Drink coconut water. These are just a few of the things I've been told since my diagnosis. I try to listen politely, thank them for their advice, and then ignore everything except what my doctor tells me to do or not do. Now let me say this: I trust my doctor and have an amazing relationship with him. I realize that not everyone is blessed with the kind of doctor that I have and not everyone has the level of trust with their doctor that I have with mine. But I would still advise that before you start or stop anything major in your life, discuss it with your doctor first. Heathy changes are a good thing. But some things need to be done in stages and not drastically so that they don't further shock your body, which is already being shocked by the treatments you are receiving. Just talk things over with your doctor before making any radical changes.

Stories about others with cancer—Heavens above, was this a common one! In the beginning it seemed like every person I talked to had to tell me about their mom or their sister or their aunt or their best friend who had breast cancer. And often the story ended with "but she died." These encounters were harder to deal with than the unsolicited advice. Sometimes it made me feel like others didn't see my cancer as a big deal. I was just another person they knew with breast cancer. Sometimes, when they told me the person had died, it was simply a discouragement.

Avoidance—Most of the folks I have talked to have had people in their lives who started avoiding them after they were diagnosed. Some people go beyond simple avoidance and completely disappear from your life. Either they don't know what to say, so they don't say anything as all, or they simply cannot handle what you're going through, for whatever reason, so they just disappear.

Ignorance is bliss—Some people go beyond just trying to avoid contact with you. They avoid acknowledging that you have cancer. On the occasions that they do see you, they avoid talking about cancer at all. They don't ask how you are feeling. They don't ask for any details about your diagnosis or prognosis. They don't ask about your treatments. They don't even acknowledge the fact that you are bald and have no eyelashes or eyebrows. They act as if nothing out of the ordinary is even going on and avoid the fact that you are, in fact, sick. Very sick.

Questions—Well, one question in particular: "How are you doing?" This question is often preceded or followed by "You look great!"—the implication being that if you don't look sick, you must not really be sick.

In each of these cases, those of us who have experienced them pretty much agree that no one says or does these things to be hurtful. Sometimes when we don't know what to say, we either say the wrong thing or we say nothing at all. And most of the time, when people give us that unsolicited advice, it's from a place of love and a desire to be helpful. And you can't be upset about that. It is all well intended, and we need to see it as such. So what do we do? We pretend. We plaster a smile on our faces, listen politely, we say thank you, and we move on. And why do we do that? Why don't we call people on it? Why don't we tell people that what they've said or how they've acted isn't helpful and is, at times, hurtful? Because we quickly learn that everyone involved, the cancer patient and the people in their lives, feels helpless. And even as we are struggling with all that we are going through, we still feel compelled to "take care of" those around us. We feel bad, but we don't want our loved ones to feel bad. So we pretend. We learn to respond to questions in a way that puts the other person at ease, even if what way isn't exactly the truth. For instance, when folks ask the dreaded "how are you doing" questions, we respond with "I'm doing really well." When they say, "You look great," we respond with "Thanks!" We learn to protect ourselves by saying "I'm fine; it's fine; everything is fine" when the truth is, nothing could be further from the truth. The truth is, often we feel horrible. Physically and mentally. We're tired. We're scared. Our bodies ache. We feel nauseated. Food tastes weird. Our hair is falling out, and not just on our heads. Our eyelashes and eyebrows are thinning or falling out completely, and we look unrecognizable to ourselves in the mirror. It's depressing, and it's hard, and it's exhausting. Anyway, the point is, we come to realize that if we say all of those things, if we tell the truth about how we're really feeling, it is upsetting to the people around us. They already feel helpless and don't know what to say, and if we tell them the whole truth about what we're experiencing, that just makes them feel worse. So we protect them. We sugar-coat our answers to their questions. We keep the worst of it to ourselves. It's easier to pretend. But our reality is that there is nothing easy about cancer and cancer treatment. It's exhausting keeping up the pretense when what we really want to do is stay in bed most of the time and moan and complain about how cruddy we feel. But we know we can't do that, so we pretend. I learned to say all the right things when people asked how I was doing. I said all the different versions of "I'm fine," and I also said all the right things as a Christian. God is so good. I can feel your prayers. I know that God is taking care of me. All of those things were, and are, true. But they didn't give an accurate picture of what I was feeling nor how I still feel sometimes. The honest response would have been "This is the hardest thing I've ever gone through, and I have lots of moment of frustration and fear. But I know that God is in the struggle with me." But I didn't say that. I didn't want people to know I was struggling. Partially because I didn't want to make people sad or make them feel sorry for me. But also because I didn't want to look like a bad Christian. I didn't want people to think that I was losing my faith in God because of cancer. Because that wasn't true either. The truth was I was struggling AND I still had faith in God. But I didn't feel like I could share that. Only a small number of people knew the whole truth. Most people only knew what I allowed them to know.

But here's the trouble with pretending: it becomes a slippery slope. Especially as a Christian. Because I was saying all the right things, I was often told things like "you are so strong" and "you are so brave." I knew better. I knew how weak I was, and that "brave" felt like a very foreign concept. And I started to feel like a complete fraud. I would often try to argue with people when they made comments like that. I would tell them they didn't see all the times that I cried or screamed or asked God why He allowed me to have cancer. But they would continue to compliment me anyway, and it felt so wrong. This was another time that guilt became a part of my story. I felt guilty for pretending to handle cancer better than I actually was. But I didn't really know what to do about it. I still had a desire to protect my loved ones from the truth of how hard it was. And I still fought the fear that if others know how great the struggle really was, they would question my faith. So I worked hard at keeping up the façade. God, however, had different plans.

About nine months into my cancer journey, I had an encounter that changed it all. I was done with chemo and had started my new routine of maintenance treatments and scans. But I was still mostly bald and still had no eyelashes or eyebrows. I had decided before I lost my hair that I would not get a wig. And scarves just didn't feel like "me." So I wore baseball caps. I had caps in every imaginable color and style, and I wore them all the time, except when I was in the privacy of my home. But my oldest nephew was getting married, and I knew that a baseball cap wasn't proper wedding attire. So I broke down and ordered an inexpensive wig. I looked through some pictures of myself and found one where I thought my hair looked good. It was long and all one length except for the bangs. And I found a wig that was very similar in style and ordered it. That was a mistake. That was not the way I had been wearing my hair at the time I was diagnosed. In fact, it was a drastic style difference. I hadn't worn my hair that long in several years, in fact. So when the wig came in and I first put it on, it was quite a shock. And not in a good way. The next day I took it to my sweet hairdresser friend along with the picture I'd used as a point of reference, and she cut and styled the wig as close to the picture as possible. I wore the wig the rest of that day, out to dinner that night with my daughter, and even out for a walk on the beach with her after dinner where we took lots of fun pictures together. It felt weird, but I assumed it was just because it was new, and I needed some time to adjust to it.

A day or two later, I had appointments for my scans, and I wore my wig to the hospital. It felt OK on my head, other than being hotter than I'd anticipated. But I was far from comfortable in it. Again, I was thinking I still just needed some adjustment time. But as I left the hospital, I ran into someone that I knew. I didn't know her well, but well enough that I instantly went into pretend mode. She asked how I was doing, and I told her I was great. I told her I was done with chemo and was starting to get past the lingering side effects from that. I told her that I was settling into my new normal of living with cancer. I told her I was adjusting to remembering to check my calendar to see when my next treatment was before committing to anything. I told her how grateful I was for all the prayers people had lifted on my behalf and how I didn't know how people who don't have a relationship with God get through things like this. I said all the right things. But in my head, all I could hear was "she knows you're wearing a wig." And I felt like a fraud. I ended the conversation and rushed to my car. As soon as I had shut the door, I pulled the sun visor down and opened the mirror and looked at myself. The bangs on my fake hair had all but rubbed off the fake eyebrows I had drawn on. And the sweat on my face from wearing that hot, fake hair was causing the glue on my fake eyelashes to let go, and one of them was already falling off. I was staring at the very picture of what the voice in my head was telling me that I was. I was a fake and a fraud. And I fell apart. I ugly-cried all the way home, rushed in the house, ripped that wig off my head, pulled the fake eyelashes off, washed what was left of my makeup off my face, put my PJs on, grabbed my computer, opened my Facebook, and composed my first, brutally honest post about living with cancer.

I still fight the urge to sugar-coat things when people ask me about my cancer. I mean, let's face it, people don't want to be around a person who is negative and whiny all the time. So I don't want to push people away by only focusing on the hard stuff. But I'm doing better about softly, carefully being more honest about what it's really like. I tell people that there are times that it's still really hard, and there are still some things that I deal with that are frustrating and difficult and are a result of my treatment meds. And I tell them that cancer has become a way of life for me. My new normal. But I also tell them how grateful I am that my cancer has responded so well to my treatment meds and has been stable for so long. I tell them how grateful I am that most of the time I feel really good. And I tell them how grateful I am for all of the blessings that God continues to pour into my life. Sometimes someone wants more details, and I am happy to share. But most of the time, this is enough. There is no pretending in that response, and that feels really good. And by the way, I never put that wig on again. And I even eventually gained the courage to post a few pictures of myself with no baseball cap on, proudly showing off my bald head.

Fear and Faith

But now thus says the Lord, he who created you,
O Jacob, he who formed you, O Israel:
"Fear not, for I have redeemed you; I have called you
by name, you are mine. When you pass through the
waters, I will be with you; and through the rivers, they
shall not overwhelm you; when you walk through
fire you shall not be burned, and the flame shall not
consume you. For I am the Lord your God,
the Holy One of Israel, your Savior.

Isaiah 43:1–3a

Behold, I have engraved you on the palms of
my hands.

Isaiah 49:16a

I remember the first time I became aware of the battle that was going on inside my head between what I was experiencing (because of cancer) and my faith in God. I feel fairly certain that I'd had this battle in my life before. The battle between dealing with difficulties in my life and how they impact my faith. In fact, I think maybe on some level, we all struggle with this from time to time. But this time I was acutely aware of it. Not just in my head, but also in my heart. It was right after I had gotten off the phone call where I learned that I did indeed have cancer and that it was breast cancer. That's all I knew at that point, but it was enough to send me instantly into this weird spiraling sensation. My thoughts and emotions were swirling around me as if they were outside of my body. I couldn't make sense of any of them. I don't remember if I was crying or not. Crying is something I do a lot of, so it wouldn't have been out of the norm for me to cry. But for some reason, I don't think I was crying in that moment. But I do remember feeling frantic. I remember frantically repeating parts of two Bible verses. I didn't quote them correctly. In fact, I think I kind of combined them into one verse. And all I could think to do was say over and over, "He knows me by name; I am engraved in the palm of His hand." I remember saying it over and over: "He know me by name; I am engraved in the palm of His hand." I was frantic to feel safe. To feel calm. To feel unafraid. Everything was spiraling out of control around me, and I was desperate to feel that calm in the midst of the storm that I'd heard about my entire Christian life. I remember not wanting to be angry. Being angry with cancer felt appropriate, but I didn't want to be angry with God. That felt enormously wrong. It felt like a betrayal. It felt non-Christian. It felt like something I should be ashamed of. But everything was just spiraling around me, and I just felt frantic.

I don't really know how long it took for that spiraling feeling to go away. But I do know this: I didn't immediately feel calm in the midst of the storm. And I felt guilty for that. I never once felt like God had abandoned me. I never once felt like He wasn't there with me. I never once felt like God wasn't real or that He didn't love me anymore. But I certainly didn't feel calm. What I felt was shame, because I felt like the things I was feeling and thinking meant I wasn't a good Christian. Fear. Confusion. Chaos. Abandonment. Dread. Darkness. Questions. Anger. These are not words we use when we describe God. He is the opposite of all of those things. Those things aren't supposed to exist in the same place as God. Right? Yet here I was, thinking and feeling all of those things, and more. Did that mean I was a bad Christian? Did that mean I wasn't really saved? Did that mean God wasn't/isn't everything I had always believed Him to be? And I was desperate to reassure myself that despite all of these things I was experiencing, despite the words I had to use to describe my thoughts and emotions, God was still there. It took me a little while. I can't tell you how long. But it wasn't that day. It wasn't the next day.

It was a process. A process of trying to figure out how faith and fear can exist in the same place. But slowly, God somehow quieted my thoughts and emotions long enough for me to realize that He was still right there, in the midst of all of the chaos, loving me just as much as He had before the second before I heard the word "cancer" for the first time. I was still just as saved while feeling all of these things as I had been before those feelings had come into being. God was still just as good and just as real and just a present as He ever had been before. And I was just as loved and saved. God created all of those emotions. He made my brain capable of thinking all of those thoughts. And to try to deny how I was feeling and what I was thinking would be lying to the very God who knows my every thought and feeling. I didn't need to feel guilty for struggling with human emotions. I needed to learn how to work through them. But I also needed to learn that I didn't need to try to hide from God while I did that. I learned to pray really honest prayers and admit to God when I was feeling scared or alone or even angry. And I learned to put aside the guilt about those emotions. I learned to give myself grace when those thoughts and feelings overwhelmed me. Because that's what God offers me. Grace. He loves me even when I'm a bundle of uncontrollable emotions or when my thoughts are irrational, or my circumstances overwhelm me. He gives me grace while I work through it, and His love never waivers. The calm came when I allowed myself to accept that faith and fear can exist in the same space. But it doesn't stay in the same space for very long. When I admit my fear to God, when I'm honest with Him about what I'm feeling, when I admit to Him that I can't handle it alone, He comes alongside me and brings with Him peace. Quiet. Calm. And my faith grows. It's a process that happens over and over. Because the fear creeps back in. The questions with no answers come back to my mind. The anger over the control that cancer still has, and will always have, over my daily life builds back up. But each time it does, and each time I get honest before God about it…again, He is faithful to carry me through the struggle…again…and restore my faith in His goodness.

Early on in my cancer journey, God brought sparrows to my mind so often. I remember my grandmother singing the song "His Eye Is on the Sparrow" when I was a little girl. It was a song I had sung many times in my life. But it took on new meaning and significance to me in the face of cancer. In the Bible, in Matthew 10, Jesus says, "Are not two sparrows sold for a penny? And not one of them will fall to the ground apart from your Father. But even the hairs of your head are all numbered. Fear not, therefore; you are of more value than many sparrows." I held tightly to these verses in those early days of my cancer journey. The words of that song and those verses from the Bible were reminders to me that God was still there and nothing was going to happen to me that was outside of God's will for me. I looked sparrows up on the internet, not so much to learn all about them, but to have a picture in my head of what a sparrow looked like. And guess what? They're some of the most plain, unexceptional-looking little birds out there. But Jesus chose those little insignificant birds to let us know that even the least of us is deeply loved, deeply seen, deeply valued by God. That was incredibly significant to me and gave me so much peace. Finally, some calm in the midst of the storm.

Another thing happened in those early days. There were so many things that I was struggling with. The sheer volume of information I had to process. The treatment schedule. The side effects from those treatments. Being bald. Trying to hold my emotions together for the sake of those around me. But I came to a realization that there was one thing about cancer that I was not struggling with. Healing. I learned very early on that my cancer does not go into remission. My cancer, at the advanced stage I am in, is not curable. My cancer battle will last the rest of my life, and likely, will be what ultimately takes my life. That's a lot to deal with. But strangely, I have not struggled with that knowledge like you would expect. Now don't get me wrong here…I still struggle! I have been angry about and questioned God about many things concerning cancer. I still do! But I have not questioned God about healing. I 100 percent believe that God CAN heal me. I 100 percent believe that God can do ANYTHING! But I also 100 percent believe that healing me from cancer is not God's plan for me. And I don't struggle with that. I can't explain that to you. I don't have an explanation. That's just how I feel.

It upsets some of my friends and family members when I say I don't believe God is going to heal me or that one day my cancer will "wake up." They don't like to hear me say things like that. I know it's because they love me and they don't want that for me. I don't want that for me either, to be quite honest. But I keep saying it out loud, and I keep it in the forefront of my thoughts for two reasons—the first one being that I don't want to be caught off guard again like I was when I was first diagnosed. I want to be prepared. I want to hit the ground running with a new treatment plan when the time comes. I want to take control of the situation when it arises, and not feel that it is controlling me the way I felt the first time. I do realize that the reality is that no matter how prepared I think I am, I will still likely be shaken when it happens. I will be scared. I will be upset. I will be angry. I will be all the things I was before. But hopefully, the next time, I won't be as overwhelmed by it. And hopefully I will be able to get my feet under me a little more quickly. But here's the second reason. I believe that God has something for me to DO with this cancer journey. I think He gives me calm and acceptance in the face of uncurable cancer because He has a plan for it that will glorify Him. And I believe that He desires for me to carry out that plan. OK, hit pause right here. I am NOT the ideal model of Christianity. I have not, and will not, ever be that person that others should strive to be. I am a hot mess. I'm a lot. I've made more mistakes than I care to admit to, and I keep messing up every single day. But guess what else I am. I am a sparrow. Small and insignificant, and yet deeply loved and cared for by God. And I believe with my whole heart that God can and does use messed-up, flawed, insignificant people and circumstances and stories to carry out His will and to point to His goodness. And I believe with my whole heart that He wants to do something good with my cancer. While I still struggle with the "why" questions, and I am still fearful of what my future cancer battle will look like, I still trust that God is doing something good with all of this. That's how I get from one day to the next. That's how I find peace. That's how I find joy. Because I believe in a good and loving God who can take something as ugly and hard as cancer and do something good with it. How can it not bring me joy that He chose to allow me to be a part of that?

Tears upon Tears

> You keep track of all my sorrows. You have collected all my tears in your bottle. You have recorded each one in your book.
>
> Psalm 56:8 (NLT)

From the moment I learned that I have cancer, I knew I would be entering a season of "hard." I did not, however, have any idea the multiple levels of hard that I was about to become intimately acquainted with. The hard began with questions. What type of cancer do I have? What stage is my cancer? What is my treatment plan? How many treatments will I have to have? Those were questions that I was able to get answers to. However, I quickly learned that sometimes getting the answer to one question raised another. I learned I have HER2+ cancer. What is HER2+ cancer? My cancer is stage IV. What does having stage IV cancer mean? And so on and so on. In the beginning, it was information overload, and it was extremely difficult to process it all. I was overwhelmed with information, and I was overwhelmed with my own emotions. It took a while to get my head wrapped around the basic facts of my diagnosis. And once I had a general understanding of the type of cancer I have and my immediate treatment plan, I thought things would get easier and that my emotions would settle down. I couldn't have been more wrong.

Treatment is the perfect example. Like most people, I had some assumptions about what it would be like, based on TV shows and movies and the little personal experience I had with friends who had gone through chemo. I thought I was in for lots of nausea and upset stomach and feeling very tired. The only part of that that was accurate for me was the very tired part. But even that wasn't like I anticipated. It was a level of exhaustion that I had never experienced before and that I honestly don't know how to explain. Often just getting out of bed to go to the bathroom or to go get something to drink felt like the most monumental task. Along with the exhaustion, I just didn't feel well. It wasn't like having the flu or any other illness I'd ever experienced. I just felt…bad. My blood pressure would dramatically drop when I would get out of bed, and several times I almost passed out. Because I was so tired and spending so much time sleeping, I wasn't drinking enough, and I would get extremely dehydrated. And dehydration made the issue with my blood pressure worse. Fortunately, those symptoms usually didn't hit until a few days after a treatment, and at first they only lasted three to four days. What I learned, though, is that with the type of chemo I was getting, side effects were cumulative. Whatever side effects I had with one treatment would happen again with the next treatment, but a little worse. So each treatment brought a little deeper level of exhaustion and feeling bad. By the end of my chemo treatments, I felt bad pretty much all the time. However, those weren't the worst of the side effects. The thing that plagued me the most was "metal mouth." Almost everything I ate tasted like metal. This is a common side effect with certain chemo drugs, and I had a pretty severe case of it. I tried all the tricks I could find on the internet or suggestions from friends who had experienced it, but nothing seemed to help me. The taste came not from the foods themselves, but from my own saliva due to the chemicals present in my body. So the more I tried to eat, the stronger the metallic taste became. When I did attempt to eat, I would eat as fast as I could, trying to get some food down before the metallic taste became unbearable and I had to stop. Most meals ended with me in tears, and still hungry. I lost a good bit of weight because I got to the point where I just didn't want to eat. I was able, after some trial and error, to find a few things that I could tolerate, and I learned what types of food to avoid. But it was such a struggle. It was important to be fueling my body so that I could tolerate the drugs that I so desperately needed, but eating became such an unpleasant, frustrating experience that I had to force myself to eat. Not only did this side effect get worse with each treatment, but it was also the only one that affected me consistently between treatments. It was also the one that took the longest to go away once I was done with chemo. To this day, years after completing chemo, there are still a few foods that I had such a bad experience with due to metal mouth that I simply cannot eat them anymore. And there are other foods, the ones that I found I was able to tolerate, that I still struggle with as well. Often when I try to eat them, I have a reaction that I can only describe as a sort of post-traumatic stress reaction. I absolutely cannot eat them on a treatment day, but even on other days, it is hit-and-miss as to whether I can eat and enjoy them. I guess it will always be that way. And it's hard.

So I survived and recovered from the hard that came with going through chemo treatments. And though it was different than what I had anticipated, I got through it. What I hadn't anticipated was all the hard that still lay ahead. I think the first real realization that difficult days, difficult seasons were still to come was when October rolled around. I had been done with chemo since early August. I was getting my energy back, most foods were tasting normal again, and I was settling into my treatment schedule. My hair was even just starting to grow again. I was still trying to come to terms with the fact that cancer was now a way of life for me, and then October hit.

It seemed that everywhere I looked there were pink ribbons. Now, for someone with breast cancer, you would think that I would embrace the pink ribbons. But not only did I not embrace them, I quickly came to resent them. Yes, they are reminders that breast cancer is a widespread issue and of the need for more research for prevention and a cure. But more often than not, pink ribbons are accompanied by stories of breast cancer survivors. Women who have been treated for and have beaten breast cancer. Their cancer stories had a beginning, a middle, and an end. That will never be my story. I will never not have cancer anymore. I will never not be in treatment. I will be a cancer patient for the rest of my life. And I got mad. Not just a little mad. Full-on angry! Every time I saw a pink ribbon, I got mad all over again. I cried angry tears. I refused to buy pink-ribbon T-shirts. I avoided Facebook posts from friends who were breast cancer survivors. I simply wanted nothing to do with anything associated with pink ribbons and was bitter about the fact that they would never be applicable to me. I began searching the internet and found that there is a ribbon specifically for those of us with metastatic breast cancer. And I found a few places where I could order T-shirts or stickers or other products with that ribbon on them. And I did order a few. I also discovered that there is one day in the month of October that is dedicated to metastatic cancer awareness. One day. October 13. And while I am glad that someone saw fit to designate a day to MBC awareness, it stung that it's just one day and it's really not even known by many people other than those directly affected by MBC. This thing that has come to define basically every aspect of who I am, the thing that everything else in my life gets scheduled around, this thing that dominates so much of my world gets one, barely acknowledged day out of a whole month dedicated to breast cancer awareness. Yet approximately 40,000 people, predominately women but a few men as well, die from breast cancer each year. And it is estimated that there are over 155,000 women and men living with MBC in the United States alone. That is only an estimate, because statistics are not collected on MBC. Those numbers have remained essentially unchanged over the last twenty years, despite advancements in treatments. And all deaths from breast cancer are caused by metastatic breast cancer. Let that soak in a second. ALL of them. And get this. It is estimated that less than 5 percent of research funding on breast cancer is spent on studying the process of metastatic breast cancer and why and how cancer spreads, despite the fact that spreading to other parts of the body is what causes breast cancer to become deadly. Yet only one day is set aside to raise awareness about MBC, and it is not publicized, and barely any funding goes into researching it. That blows my mind and breaks my heart. They say that knowledge is power. But in my case, this knowledge is hard. I don't get as angry now when October comes as the world around me is flooded with pink ribbons to celebrate those who have survived a disease that I will never stop fighting. But they are still painful reminders, and I still refuse to wear them. I pull out my MBC ribbon shirts during October and wear those defiantly. But I've made the choice not to wear them often during the rest of the year. It's hard enough to have the notifications pop up on my phone every three weeks, reminding me that it's time for treatment again, as if I needed to be reminded. It's hard enough to work on not talking about my cancer as often as I think about it. It's hard enough to try to control the scary thoughts about what my future could hold because of cancer. So I choose not to wear my "ribbon" T-shirts often so that I don't have that reminder in my line of vision as well. Because it's hard.

Another area of hard that I quickly became acquainted with is the change in the dynamics of many of my relationships. When I was first diagnosed, I wasn't prepared for range of responses I would receive from people. I was kind of prepared for the sympathy I got. Most people were so kind and encouraging. And that was incredibly helpful. Particularly on the days that I felt the worst or was struggling with my emotions. God always saw to it that someone reached out to me in some way right at the moment that I needed it the most. But I wasn't surprised by that. I was grateful. I was humbled. But I wasn't surprised. God has placed some incredible people in my life because He knew I was going to need them to help me through life. And His faithfulness in that was never more evident than while I was going through chemo. He knew who

I would need and what I would need, and He prompted my family and friends to provide for each of those needs. They were, and continue to be, the hands and feet of Jesus in my life. But what did catch me off guard were the people in my life who simply disappeared. I've already touched on this briefly in the previous chapter. But it was painful enough, hard enough, that it bears repeating. My head knows the likely reasons most of them chose to disappear from my life. Some didn't know what to say, so they said nothing at all. Some couldn't handle the fears that being around me stirred up in them. Some couldn't handle the seriousness of my illness and were not prepared to deal with human mortality. I'm sure there are many more reasons why people check out of the lives of others at times when they are actually needed most. But regardless of the reasons why, it's painful. Some of those friends who were silent during those first few difficult months of my cancer journey have since come back into my life. I'm grateful for that, but I can't say that things are necessarily the same as they were before. I don't love them any less than I did before. But the dynamics of our friendship have changed. Probably forever. Some who quietly slipped out of my life during that time have remained absent from my life. That's hard on a different level. I know that some friendships/relationships are just for a season, and so I have to accept that our season is over. But that doesn't mean that I don't miss them. It doesn't make me wonder any less why they chose to pull away. It doesn't make the void that they left any less lonely. But God has sent a new people into my life and into my heart to walk this journey alongside me in a way that no one else could. He knew what and who I would need long before I even felt the need. What a gift!

Some of the people that God has brought into my life have been ladies who are or were also battling cancer. I have said that having cancer is like being in a club you never asked to join. But there is strange and immense relief in having the opportunity to have a conversation with someone who is also living it or has lived it. There's no need to explain the medical terms. There's no need to put on a brave face. There's no need to sugar-coat anything. They just get it. These people fit into one of three categories: "have lived it," "are currently living it," or "will live with it the rest of their lives." Those are very different things, and each comes with a set of emotions that are sometimes difficult for me to navigate. Regardless of these categories, the conversations we have about what it's like, how hard it is, how exhausting the experience is of going through treatment, are pretty similar. Most women who have had or do have breast cancer go through chemo, and we all have hard stories to share about that experience. Even though some of what we've gone through is quite different, and the degree to which we've been hit with side effects and such can also be quite different, there is still this overwhelming sense of connection and understanding we feel with each other. But the emotions I struggle with stem from what differentiates what category they are in.

For those in the "are currently living it" category, I feel such sympathy and empathy. I want to help them through it. I want to share my story in hopes that they will feel less alone and maybe even find some hope and encouragement. But it's hard when I know that they will likely come to the end of their journey and once they heal from the disease and the treatment, they will likely move on and cancer will be a chapter of their lives that has reached its conclusion. They will move from the "are currently living with it" category to the "lived it" category. While most of me looks forward to being able to celebrate that with them, looks forward to cheering for them when they ring the "done with treatment" bell, there's a little part of me that is jealous. They will eventually get to talk about cancer in the past tense, and their life's journey will take a turn into cancer-free days. That won't be me. I won't ever ring that bell. I won't ever be cancer free. Cancer won't ever be past tense for me. I won't ever move into that "lived it" category. And it's hard.

Now the "will live with it the rest of their lives" category is where I fit in. These are my people. These are the ones who understand me from the second we share that we are stage IV. These are the people that I know I need to love with urgency. Now. While I can. But this is where I struggle the most with the fact that I feel that God has called me to minister to others in their cancer journeys. I learned all too quickly that being emotionally connected to others with stage IV cancer means having to be mentally prepared for things that I don't want to be mentally prepared for. I learned that I have to be willing to accept that I will not have answers for all of the questions that come with loving people and knowing the stories and struggles of people who are battling this horrible disease. I can't explain why my cancer has responded so well to my treatment meds while other people have to jump from one treatment plan to another, sometimes multiple times, because their cancer didn't respond to or stopped responding to the very same meds that I'm on. How do I celebrate how well I'm doing right now and not feel guilty when someone else gets a scan report that says her cancer is progressing and that they are quickly coming the end of their treatment options for her? How do I find the courage to continue to be present in the journeys of others, knowing that there is a very real possibility that I will have to say goodbye to them when they lose their battle with this monster? How do I continue to encourage them to have faith in a good God who loves them beyond description while they battle cancer with everything in them and still feel their life slipping away? How do I not lose my faith as I watch it happen over and over, and each time know that I am likely getting a glimpse into my own future? These are questions that I will never have answers to. And it's hard.

Hard for me usually means tears. Tears upon tears. I've always been an emotional person. I cry a lot. It's kind of a joke among my friends and family. I was once sharing a story with a friend about something I'd been through, and at one point in the story I said, "And I cried." Immediately she said, "Well, duh! It's you!" We laughed about it, and I think about that often. I don't think anyone who knows me even moderately well is surprised when I tear up in their presence. I really do cry a lot. But I got it from my precious Momma. Daddy used to jokingly say that if he took my mom to see a movie and she'd heard that it was sad, she would start crying when he bought the tickets. That always makes me laugh. But like my sweet Momma, I do feel deeply and respond with tears in many circumstances. Not just sad situations. I cry when I'm frustrated. I cry when I'm scared. I cry when I'm really angry. But I also cry when I'm extremely happy, when I'm deeply touched, and when I'm really excited. And I'm fairly certain I have cried each of those types of tears over cancer. Without a doubt I have cried tears of sadness and frustration and fear and anger over cancer. But I cried with happiness when I finished chemo. I cried because of how touched I was at the outpouring of love I received when I was first diagnosed. I cried tears of excitement when I got my first scan report stating that my cancer was considered stable. I've cried those tears over my own cancer. But I've also cried all of those types of tears as I've shared in the cancer journey of other people. I'm certain there will be countless more tears to come in the days ahead, both for myself and for others. And I believe with everything in me that none of those tears went unnoticed by my Father in heaven. I believe that when I cry happy tears, He rejoices over me. And I believe that when I cry bitter tears, He feels my pain and loves me through it. Right now, while I'm still walking this journey, I will trust that He is with me every second. I am promised that He is over and over in His Word.

Isaiah 41:10 says, "Fear not, for I am with you; be not dismayed, for I am your God; I will strengthen you, I will help you, I will uphold you with my righteous right hand.".

Isaiah 43:1–3 says, "…Fear not, for I have redeemed you; I have called you by name, you are mine. When you pass through the waters, I will be with you; and through the rivers, they shall not overwhelm you; when you walk through fire you shall not be burned, and the flame shall not consume you. For I am the Lord your God, the Holy One of Israel, your Savior…"

Romans 8:38–39 says, "For I am sure that neither death nor life, nor angels nor rulers, nor things present nor things to come, nor powers, nor height nor depth, nor anything else in all creation, will be able to separate us from the love of God in Christ Jesus our Lord."

And these are just three of many places He promises to be with me. But I am also promised that the day will come when I will not cry anymore. Not in sadness or fear or frustration or anger. Maybe I will still cry with joy and rejoicing when I am in heaven with my Savior for eternity. But I won't cry in sadness anymore. Because cancer will be a thing of my past. I won't have any more questions that I don't have answers to. I won't struggle anymore. I won't have to say goodbye to anyone else who has lost a battle with cancer, or any other disease or illness. There won't be any more hard.

Revelation 21:4 says, "He will wipe away every tear from their eyes, and death shall be no more, neither shall there be mourning, nor crying, nor pain anymore, for the former things have passed away."

So for now, I may continue to shed tears upon tears. And that's OK. Because "Those who sow in tears shall reap with shouts of joy!" (Psalm 126:5) and "Weeping may tarry for the night, but joy comes with the morning" (Psalm 30:5b).

Questions with No Answers

> But he said to me, "My grace is sufficient for you, for my power is made perfect in weakness." Therefore, I will boast all the more gladly of my weaknesses, so that the power of Christ may rest upon me."
>
> 2 Corinthians 12:9

Dealing with cancer, no matter where you are in the process, is difficult. And how a person handles their cancer experience is very unique to each individual. Much like how people cope with grief in different ways and on different timetables, people with cancer tend to have their own unique ways and timetables in how they cope with their diagnosis, treatments, side effects, and life beyond cancer. But learning to live with cancer for the rest of your life is a whole different monster, with its own unique challenges. Again, each person has to figure out for themselves how to cope. For me personally, I'm still a work in progress. I can look back and see how much I have changed in how I approach daily life with cancer, but it is often still a one-step-forward/two-steps-back kind of thing for me. In the beginning, thoughts of cancer consumed and overwhelmed me. It was often debilitating, and I shed a lot of tears and spent a lot of time just trying to come to terms with the fact that having cancer was now my life. Or that's how it felt at the time. That cancer was now what my whole life was about. Now, although there is still not a single day that goes by that I don't think about cancer, it doesn't consume me the way it used to. Well, not most days anyway. I still have days, sometimes a few days, where something will trigger the fear/frustration/anger about cancer, and I spend a little time wallowing in the self-pity pit. When that happens, though, I've learned to give myself the grace and not feel guilty about having times when I'm overwhelmed by cancer and to just let myself cry it out. Then, I pull myself together and get on with life. But it took me a while to get to that place where I can better manage those hard days. It took me a while to give myself grace in those times and not feel weak or small or like a failure. Grace to admit that it is hard. Grace to say sometimes it's OK to not be OK. But also learning to have the strength to not stay in that place. Strength to pull myself out of the pit. Strength to refocus my thoughts from the hard to the blessings. Strength to redirect my thoughts from the "what its" of my future with cancer and instead focus my thoughts on all the things I have to look forward to in my life. The hard days, the struggles still happen. But they're less and less frequent, and I've learned how to better manage when they do happen. It has been and continues to be a process.

One of the things that helps me is to look back at how differently I handle some things now versus how I handled them early on. Like cancer anniversaries. The anniversary of the first time I heard the words "you have cancer." The anniversary of my first appointment with my precious oncologist. The anniversary of getting my official diagnosis. The anniversary of my first treatment. And the anniversary of my last chemo treatments. Those dates used to fill me with anxiety. They were all dates that signified the start of my new life. Usually when someone talks about having new life, it's a positive thing. But for me, it's about moving from my BC (before cancer) life, and my now AC (after cancer diagnosis) life. Not a "new life" I ever would have chosen. So for the first few AC years, I dreaded those dates. They filled me with anxiety, and I would think back through every detail of those events. I would get very sad and would really struggle with my emotions. Then, the strangest thing happened…the third anniversary of my initial diagnosis came and went without me even remembering! I remembered the day after, and was shocked that the significance of the day had completely escaped me the day before. I was so proud of myself! And even when I did remember, I didn't get upset about it. I was even more proud of that! That is one of the two anniversaries that I'd struggled with the most. But since then, somehow, although it is still a very significant thing in my life, I no longer spiral into a dark place about it. It's certainly won't ever be a day that I celebrate. But I'm proud of myself that my emotions no longer spiral out of control because of it.

The other anniversary that I have struggled with is the day of my last chemo treatment. Weird, huh? You would think that would be a day to celebrate. And for most cancer patients, it is. But I'm not a typical cancer patient. On the five-year anniversary of my last chemo treatment, I found myself in a very strange place with my emotions and my thoughts. I didn't know what to think or feel about that today. I felt like I should be feeling something out of the ordinary. Should I have wanted to celebrate? I didn't. Should I have felt angry that chemo didn't cure me? I wasn't. I knew all along that it wouldn't. Should I have felt sad? I didn't. Not particularly. So how should I have felt?

I remember a few things about August 6, 2018. But I remember more about the week leading up to that day. I was really struggling. I was so physically exhausted from all my body had been through at that point. And I was mentally and emotionally exhausted as well. I was so weary of the whole thing. The cancer, the poison that was fighting the cancer, the fear, the anger, the questions, and the side effects. Have mercy, I was weary of the side effects! They had gotten worse with each treatment, and I had decided I was going to tell my doctor that I wasn't going to have that last chemo treatment. I just didn't think I had the strength to do it even one more time. Thank goodness God knew I was going to get to that point, and He put me in a room with a group of people who prayed over me and sang over me and literally breathed life back into me. And I did have that last treatment, and I'm grateful I did.

But another thing I was struggling with was the bell. The bell that people ring when they have completed treatment. I had seen the gathering of the nurses and sometimes doctors around a person who had just had their last treatment. I had seen them applaud and hug that person after they joyfully rang that bell. I had seen the smiles of the family members there to witness this moment. And I had seen the tentative smiles of patients as they rang the bell. And I wanted no part of it. See, that bell represented the end. The finish line. The closing of a chapter. Ringing out the old life of cancer and chemo. Ringing in the new life of no cancer and chemo. And that was not my life. Yes, I was having my least chemo treatment, but in three weeks, I would be back there, in that same building, in that same chair (my favorite nurse always saved it for me), getting most of the same drugs I was having on that last chemo day. Yes, chemo was ending, and along with it, a handful of the pre-meds to help fight the side effects. But I would still have treatment every three weeks. I would still see my oncologist every three weeks. I would still have to schedule my life around treatments every three weeks. I would still get the Thursday and Saturday email and text reminders that I had treatment on

Monday. Every. Three. Weeks. After that last chemo treatment, I would still have cancer.

But there was something else. There was something that I had seen in the faces of a few people I had witnessed ringing that bell. There was a timidness in the way they rang it. There was still a touch of fear behind their eyes. There was usually a hesitation in ringing that bell with confidence and boldness. Was it fear that the chemo hadn't killed it all? Was it fear that it would come back? Was it just sheer exhaustion from all they'd endured? Was it guilt that they were ringing the bell in the midst of a room full of people who were, at that moment, having chemo pumped into their bodies? I don't know the answers to any of those questions. I just know that I sensed something that made me...something. Sad? Angry? Jealous? I don't know exactly. I just know I didn't want any part of that bell!! I asked my nurses not to even mention, to me or anyone else around me, that I was having my last chemo treatment. Because the truth is, I have no idea if I've had my last chemo treatment. I had my last of the first round of chemo. But I have no idea when or if I'll have more. But I know the statistics. I know the very real possibilities. I know the nature of this stupid cancer I have and will always have. No end to it. No cure for it. So no bell for me. Not that day. Not ever. No bell.

Even as I remembered all of that on that fifth anniversary, I wasn't upset about it. I didn't feel like celebrating the anniversary of my last chemo treatment. But I wasn't really struggling with my own cancer that day either. I was feeling rather introspective. That's a big word for me, and I looked it up to make sure I am using it correctly. "Introspection" is defined as the examination or observation of one's own mental and emotional processes. So I guess that's the right word for what I was doing on that weird anniversary day. I was thinking about, asking myself questions about how I process some things that were currently happening. Not things that were happening directly to me. But happening to people around me. I was trying to figure out how to process what was happening to others and how it impacted me, without it appearing that I was trying to make the struggles of others all about me. I was trying to navigate being empathetic with the circumstances of others while fighting against letting myself spiral into a dark place. Because witnessing how cancer was hurting people around me that I know and love is difficult. I was trying to figure out how to minister to them, comfort them, encourage them, which I feel called to do and deeply desire to do, without allowing their struggles to stir up my own struggles. This is something I have continued to struggle with and still have no easy answers for. Questions with no answers are hard for me. For instance, why do cancer drugs help some but not others? Why are some people hit with wave after wave of bad news about their cancer while others respond incredibly well to their treatments? Why do people have cancer in the first place? No answers.

Some people say that they believe that "they" already have a cure for cancer. But that curing cancer isn't lucrative so "they" keep it secret so "they" can still make millions, billions off the suffering of cancer patients. I certainly don't want to believe the world is that cruel! But could that be true? No answers.

I've heard it said, and I've said it myself, that two people can have an almost identical diagnosis and yet their cancer battles will not look anything alike. Where one responds well to treatment, the other does not. And there's no explanation for that. It just all depends on your body. That's crazy to me! Yet I know it's true. I've seen it. I've experienced it personally. But why is that? No answers.

I have watched several precious ladies walk with grace through what can only be described as hellish battles with breast cancer. Each of them just happened to also have metastatic breast cancer, and one of those has an almost identical diagnosis to mine. Each of these ladies has now lost their battle with cancer and are in heaven now, completely healed. But while they were fighting against this horrible monster, I would often find myself asking, "why her?" That's a horrible trap to fall into. My heart said, "She is such a precious, good, Jesus-loving woman! Why does God allow HER to have cancer?" So what was I saying? Only "bad" people should be allowed to have cancer? WHAT??? Do I really think that??? No. I don't. That would mean mercy and grace aren't real. And I completely believe in mercy and grace!! With my whole heart. So that question shouldn't even cross my mind. Yet I found myself asking, "Why her, God? She loves you so much, but you're letting her go through this horrific battle, hit with blow after blow of bad news. I don't get it!!!" No answers.

And then I find myself asking another why question: why me? Why has God allowed my cancer to respond so well to treatment? Why has He kept mine stable long past what is typical for this type of cancer? Why am I doing so well when others are not? I know it's not because I "deserve" it. My friends don't deserve bad news any more than I deserve good news. It doesn't work that way. So how does it work??? WHY? No answers.

And then another question. A "how" question. How do I show love and support and encouragement to these precious people when I am doing so well while they are facing new struggles seemingly everywhere they look? Do I back away because I feel guilty that I'm doing well? If I try to show empathy, will they resent me? Do I pray quietly in the background for fear of it causing them pain if I tell them I'm praying for them? We all know I didn't make the decision for my cancer to respond well to treatment while theirs hasn't. We all know I didn't choose for one of my friends to be diagnosed with a new kind of cancer, different and unrelated to what she's already beaten. I'm not in control of my own cancer, let alone theirs. So how do I help? How do I encourage? How do I love? And how do I do any of those without it causing them additional pain because I'm doing well, and they are not? So many questions. No answers.

One of my friends that I've lost once told me that when she read my posts on my cancer Facebook page about getting great scan reports, she felt jealous. She didn't say it with bitterness. She didn't say it in a mean or snarky way. Just stated it. And I felt horrible. I didn't know what to say. I'd been so focused on hoping that my positive scan results would give hope to someone else who'd been diagnosed with MBC (See! You CAN live with MBC!) that I'd never stopped to think about how my continued stability might feel to someone who keeps getting bad news practically every time they have scans. I'd never stopped to think of the "why" questions my good scan results might bring to the mind of someone who just got scary scan reports. "Why DC? Why has her cancer been stable for so long, yet mine is still growing and spreading? Why did the first meds she tried work so well for her, and I'm having to switch to new drugs…again? Why her and not me? Why me and not her?" And I didn't know what to say. Ouch. Guilt. No explanation.

And what about my friend who passed away after a fourteen-year battle after a diagnosis almost identical to mine? See, she's the only one I've personally known so far with my exact same kind of cancer. But her battle was so much more brutal than mine has been so far. She was good about posting updates on Facebook. She was SO good about praising God for letting her live as long as she had after her diagnosis. She was always so encouraging and positive and grateful and faithful. But she was also pretty honest about what her battle looked like, what the treatment plan was, and how she was feeling. And I found that many times I would start to read an update and I couldn't finish it. It scared me. I couldn't help but think, "Is this a glimpse into my own future??" And I just couldn't!! Most times I would go back after a while and finish reading it. But sometimes it was days later. And in the meantime, I'm ashamed to say, I tried my best not to think about her. And in not thinking about her, I didn't pray for her. GUILT!!!! Especially since I am confident that she prayed for me often. But there's the ugly truth. Sometimes I hid behind my fear of possibly seeing what my future with cancer could look like, and in doing so I didn't go to the throne of God on her behalf. Selfish. Guilt. Shame. All things that I have battled since her death. And even more guilt because I am certain that if I'd had the opportunity to confess all of this to her, she would have not only forgiven me, but would have probably completely understood, and would have turned my confession into an opportunity to encourage and minister to me. That's who she was.

I guess that's why I was so void of emotions about that five-year anniversary. Because in the great scheme of things, what that anniversary represented didn't matter. What mattered to me then and what matters to me right now is being introspective. Trying to figure out how to process the emotions that inevitably come while trying to come alongside and support and encourage others in their cancer battles while still dealing with my own. How to be empathetic without letting my own emotions swallow me up. How to encourage others who must fight so fiercely while I am still responding so well to treatment

Friends, people who reach out to me through my cancer Facebook page…struggling…battling…afraid…frustrated…tired…questioning…what do I say to them? Is there any way for me, who is doing well, to be an encouragement to them as they struggle? Do my efforts to be empathetic and supportive actually cause them more pain? Do my posts about good scan reports feel like a knife in the back to them? How do I deal with wanting to celebrate good news I receive while feeling guilty when others don't? It's a hard place to be. People frequently stop themselves when they're sharing their burdens with me and say things like "But this is nothing compared to what you deal with!" And that makes me sad for them. I tell them not to compare. That hard is hard and we are supposed to bear each other's burdens. And I can't do that if they're afraid to share with me because their "hard" isn't cancer. Yet I find myself caught in a similar trap sometimes. Do I reach out to a friend who is having a horrible battle with cancer to try to be supportive and encouraging, knowing that they could resent the fact that my body has responded well and my cancer is stable? And how do I minister to others without being overwhelmed with thoughts of "is this what my future holds" creeping in? No answers.

So what do I do? This is one question that I do have an answer to. Pray. It's all I can do. I can pray. And I can ask you all to pray. Pray for the precious people that God places in our lives and that we love dearly. God knows their battles and their struggles and their needs. Maybe it's not cancer. Maybe it's some other battle that they face. We all have people in our lives who are facing things that are hard. So please pray for these precious people as they travel the path that God had laid before them. Pray for healing and comfort and peace. And please pray for their families and friends as they walk through their struggles with them.

There always seems to be a lot to try to figure out. There always seems to be a lot to process. There are always questions with no answers. There is a lot that I don't now and never will figure out. But this I know: God has given me the opportunity to do something good with my cancer journey. He's given me the desire to reach out to others who are fighting this horrible thing and to share my heart with them and try to encourage them and give them some hope. And even though it's sometimes hard, I'm still committed to trying my best to be a help to others. So I am choosing to rest in II Corinthians 12:9: "But he said to me, 'My grace is sufficient for you, for my power is made perfect in weakness.' Therefore, I will boast all the more gladly of my weaknesses, so that the power of Christ may rest upon me." And I am going to try to give myself some grace when I feel weak or powerless or inadequate for the task that He has given me. And I will trust that He will bless my meager, bumbling efforts. I will trust that He will use them for His purpose and for His glory. For those who are battling, let me share with you the words to a song by After Grace called "Easy Answers." This is who I want to be for those in my life who are facing battles, and more importantly, I want you all to know that this is who God ALWAYS is for you!

I'm not gonna tell you things will be OK
Everything happens for a reason
You just need a little faith
Cause I know how the word felt
On my darkest day
When people who meant well
Only bruised me with cliches
Doesn't leave me much to speak
As time goes by you'll see

I'm here to be a safe place
Where you can scream your fears
Let your heart fall apart
I'm a shoulder for your tears
And until some light appears

I'll stand here in your darkness
I'll hold you up in prayer
I'll sit with you in silence
I'm not going anywhere
We can wrestle with the mystery
Of what God has in mind
Together we will find
His love goes beyond hard times…
And easy answers

Change

> **Jesus Christ is the same yesterday and today and forever.**
>
> Hebrews 13:8

> **The Lord is trustworthy in all he promises and faithful in all he does.**
>
> Psalm 145:13b NIV

I heard a saying many years ago that has come back to my mind often: the only thing you can truly count on is change. Although there is a lot of truth in that statement, it doesn't change the fact that I don't do well with change. We all have to learn to adapt as we go through life and our circumstances change. But I'm finding that the older I get, the harder change is for me. And I went through a short period of time where there were several changes in my little world that were difficult for me. And, as I'm sure you've already guessed, they had to do with my cancer.

I arrived at treatment one day and learned that my favorite nurse had moved to a new position that would allow her more flexibility and more time with her daughter. While I was thrilled for her, losing her was very hard for me. It was the second time in my cancer journey that I had lost my primary treatment nurse. And it was just plain hard for me. See, my port is extremely personal to me. It's in the right side of my chest and has a tube that runs into my jugular vein and into my heart. And I've come to view it as my lifeline. It's how I've always received the meds that killed some of my cancer and keeps the remaining cancer in check. It's a big deal. And to access that port, a nurse has to get pretty up close and personal, so I don't want just any random chemo nurse to access it. Some people seem to be fine with having a different nurse each time they go to treatment. I am not one of those people. I want a nurse that I can connect with. I want a nurse that I can build a relationship with. I want to know that at least 90 percent of the time, when I go into that treatment center, I am going to be taken care of by the same person. And furthermore, I want to be in the same section and, if possible, the same chair in the treatment each time. I like a quiet corner chair where there's not a lot of traffic back and forth in front of me. All the activity makes an already-stressful situation even more stressful for me. But the next few treatments after "my" nurse left, not only did I have a different nurse each time, but I was also never again in "my" chair or even in "my" section of the treatment center. And it was incredibly stressful for me. But the day I learned that my favorite nurse was leaving, I had a precious lady that took care of me. I had met her several weeks prior and had immediately fallen in love with her. And she was right there with me when I learned that "my" nurse wasn't there that day and that she was moving to a new job. She was so compassionate and understanding about why it shook me up so badly. And she even understood about why it was upsetting to me to be in a different part of the treatment center. She was just…precious. But I knew that she wouldn't become "my" nurse, because she was just at this center for training before moving to a brand-new treatment center, in the same hospital system but across town. So the next time I went to treatment, I was filled with anxiety, because I had no idea who my nurse would be. When I was called from the waiting room, sure enough, it was a nurse that I had seen many times walking through the center, but I had never had any encounter with her other than a polite hello. I have zero complaints about her capabilities as a nurse. Zero. But…she was so different than what I was accustomed to. I wasn't allowed to choose where I sat, and I was in a pretty high-traffic, kind of noisy location right in front of the nurses' station. I had to keep telling myself to stay calm. But each little thing that was different sent new waves of anxiety through me. Even though I got through with treatment rather quickly that day, by the time I left, I was exhausted from the effort it took to stay calm. I continued to have different nurses each week for a while and continued to struggle with anxiety over the lack of consistency.

Since being diagnosed and beginning this new lifestyle of living with cancer, I've noticed that I've gotten more sensitive to change. Particularly when it has to do with cancer or cancer treatments. A lot of people would not have had a second thought about having different nurse for fir each treatment. So why did it have such a negative impact on me? Why does it throw me into a tailspin to have a PA walk in an exam room verses the doctor I was anticipating seeing? That has happened to me multiple times, and each time it has been upsetting to me. It was happening most often with one particular doctor, even after I requested that I only see her. But it still continued to happen. The first two times, a nurse came in and told me that the doctor was running behind and that I could either wait for the doctor or I could see the PA. I elected to wait. And when I made my next appointment, I would ask again to ONLY be scheduled to see the doctor and not the PA. A couple of appointments went by without incident, but then it happened again. This time, however, the PA herself came in and basically announced that I was seeing her instead of the doctor. I was stunned and intimidated, so I said nothing. As the appointment went on, I got more and more frustrated and upset. It was obvious that she had not taken the time to learn anything about me and hadn't read notes from my previous appointments. As she glanced quickly at my chart while she was talking to me, she asked me if I was still having a problem with insomnia. I told her that I was. She then proceeded to lay out suggestions of things she thought I should try before we tried any sort of medication to help me sleep, and that if none of those things helped, then we would discuss medication and my next appointment. That's all well and good, and I have a lot of respect for a doctor, or PA as the case may be, who tries to help without immediately jumping to just writing a prescription. The problem was, I had had the identical conversation with my doctor at my previous visit. All the things that the PA suggested I try, I had already tried at the suggestion of my doctor, a year prior to that visit. When I told her that, she said, "Oh, I see that now." Frustration!

After that visit, my anxiety level about seeing someone other than my regular doctor or other medical professional went through the roof. It happened at physical therapy, and I got so upset that I almost didn't stay for my therapy session. It happened at my ophthalmologist's office, and I cried all the way home afterward. And it even happened at my beloved oncologist's office. I happen to love the PA that works with my oncologist. But I was getting scan results that day, and my oncologist and I had agreed that he would always be the one to give me scan results. So when she walked in instead of my oncologist, I almost fell apart. My results were good, she was sweet, the appointment itself was uneventful. But I wasn't anticipating nor emotionally prepared to see her, so it sent me into a tailspin. I had to stop in the restroom after leaving the office and before heading downstairs for my treatment appointment, because I needed to cry for a minute. But even after crying a bit, I just couldn't shake it. I cried off and on through the three-plus hours I sat in the treatment chair that day. I was so shaken up by it that I just couldn't pull myself together fully until I left the building that day and really let myself have a good cry in my car.

After each of these events, and once I got my emotions in check about them, I was able to talk to my physical therapist, the scheduling coordinator at my eye specialist's office, and my oncologist about what had happened and how it had upset me. Each one treated me with much compassion and made notes in my chart that I was not to see anyone but "my" person for future appointments. And after the encounter with PA at that other doctor's office, I got permission from my oncologist to stop seeing her once a year and just maintain an as-needed relationship there. Although I was relieved with how each of those situations was ultimately resolved, it made me do some reflecting about why these encounters upset me so badly in the first place. The conclusion I came to came down to one word: relationship. Having a chronic illness, ongoing treatments, and side effect from the illness itself and from the treatments usually comes with having a lot of medical appointments and medical professionals in your life. Mine is no exception. A few have just been temporary, small things that have popped up and necessitated a visit or two with a particular doctor. But those were short-lived, and I didn't have the time nor the need to develop a real doctor/patient relationship. But there are other circumstances in my life that require multiple appointments. Some for a few months, some for the rest of my life. And in those circumstances, I want to be with someone that I can develop a real relationship with. I want to be with someone who actually knows me, knows my health situation without me having to tell the story all over again each time I come in for an appointment. I want to be seen as a person and not just a random patient briefly passing through a practice. I want to have complete trust that the person providing my care is partnering with me in this lifelong journey that cancer has forced me into. I want to be with someone who isn't going to label me as high-maintenance or an overreactor when I have big emotions about what my body is going through. It's about relationship. Not about being passed around to whoever happens to be available at the moment. And not about someone else choosing for me who is responsible for my care. I get to make that choice. I get to have a say-so. And once that choice is made, once I have a connection and a relationship with and have built trust with someone, that is the someone I want to see when I come to an appointment. And it's not about the letters after their name. My primary care doctor is a PA. My physical therapist was a DPT. A person doesn't have to have "MD" after their name for me to completely trust in their ability to care of me. But they do have to treat me like a real person. They do have to respect my right to choose for myself who I place my trust in, and they must be willing to earn that trust. They do have to treat me like a partner in my health plan. They do have to have compassion for the fact that this is hard. And they do have to respect the fact that, although I am fully capable of talking intelligently with them about what is going on with my body, I also have lots of emotions about it, and they do have to respect that it is OK for me to express those emotions. It's all about relationship for me. And I try very hard to always choose those doctors and other medical professionals who also want it to be about a relationship. These are the people that I choose to be a part of my healthcare team.

This event of losing my nurse and ultimately spending some time reflecting about why change affected me as profoundly as it does started just before the Christmas holidays. Over the next several weeks, I also did some reflecting about other changes in my life and how they've affected me. And I had an eye-opening revelation. There had been a drastic change that had taken place in my life that I hadn't even really recognized.

And it had to do with beginning a new year. Growing up, we never really did any of the New Year's Eve stuff that a lot of people do. We didn't stay up late or have a party, or any of those kinds of things. I'm not sure why. We just didn't. And I haven't as an adult either. Parties are just not my "thing." But we've always had a traditional, Southern meal on New Year's Day: pork of some sort, rice, black-eyed peas, greens of some sort, and corn bread. Again, I've followed that tradition as an adult. And even though we never had a big celebration to bring in the new year, having the tradition of that meal has always made it feel like a special day for me. Until cancer. As I said, I can't say that until I had a reason to do some reflecting about change that I'd been acutely aware that my view had changed. But then it hit me that on January 1, 2024, although I made my traditional new year's meal, the only reason it felt special is because we also took the opportunity to celebrate my middle child's birthday (which is January 2) since the whole family was able to be together. But strangely, it didn't feel like a new year was beginning to me. It just felt like an ordinary day. Now don't get me wrong. I am not a person who makes a bunch of resolutions or has the whole "new year = new me" mentality. I know myself better than that. I'm the same Donna Carole on January 1 as I was pretty much every other day of the previous year. Sure, there are a lot of things that start fresh with the new year: new tax year, new insurance deductible to meet, new semester of college for my youngest, new HOA fees to pay…fun stuff like that. But I'm pretty much the same DC year in and year out. So if nothing about celebrating "New Year's" has changed, then why do I feel differently about it? Simple. Cancer.

See, since February 11, 2018, pretty much everything about the passing of time for me has become related to cancer. From the time the actual new year begins, I find myself dwelling on the events that happened between January 1, 2018, and February 11, 2018. I look back at pictures or posts about things that were going on in that brief window of time between when the new year began, and I was blissfully unaware that I was sick, and that Sunday when I went to the ER in horrific pain and learned that I had cancer that had already spread throughout my body. Those few weeks now seem like this disconnected span of days that don't mark the beginning of 2018, but rather mark the end of life before cancer. It's like that chunk of time isn't really related to anything that came before it or after it. It's just those days leading up to February 11, 2018. And that's where the change happened. My "new year" no longer begins on Jan 1. It begins on February 11. Now, every February 11, I will be acutely aware of how long it has been since I first heard the words "you have cancer." And I will remember many of the things that happened over about a three-week period that redefined my future. I will remember that I was told that the drugs they were going to use to treat my cancer could give me ten or more years to live. Sadly, my brain tends to focus on the ten years versus the "or more" part. Which means that on February

11 I will be acutely aware of how many of the ten years have passed since February 11, 2018. February 11 will mark the beginning of another year of living with, battling with, struggling with, being held captive by cancer. My new year brings with it questions like "how much longer do I have to live?" and "is this the year my cancer wakes up?" I want to focus on the positives that I am aware of. Like the fact that most people with a similar diagnosis have not gone as long as I have at this point without a reoccurrence. Most people with a similar diagnosis have not responded as well to treatment as I have. Most people with a similar diagnosis aren't doing as well as I am at this point in their journey. I truly do have much to be thankful for, and I know I am tremendously blessed. I don't take any of that for granted. But. It is extraordinarily difficult not to go through life feeling like I have an expiration date stamped on my head and it's getting closer and closer. Yes, I know that we all have an expiration date. Yes, I know that only God knows when and how we will leave this world. Yes, I do believe that God is in complete control, and I do have complete faith in His love for me. But I also know that God created all of these emotions that I am experiencing, and to pretend that I'm not struggling with them would be to lie to God and to lie to you. And I'm just not going to do that. So on New Year's Day, 2024, I was acutely aware that February 11 was coming fast, and I was feeling all kinds of ways about it.

As always, in the midst of the hard, God has been so faithful to send me blessings that are impossible to ignore. In the afternoon of January 1, 2024, I learned that my daughter was expecting another baby. That certainly added a bright spot to that otherwise ordinary-feeling day. We later learned that she would be having another little boy. On January 5, 2024, my daughter-in-law delivered a second baby girl. Two little girls and two little boys. My heart is full to overflowing! If you know me at all, you know I'm CRAZY in love with my grandbabies! So welcoming another little girl into our world and anticipating the arrival of another little boy coming later in the year did bring a great deal of happiness to the otherwise hard moments I typically experience surrounding the anniversary of my diagnosis. And as it turned out, the start of the new year also ushered in some other positive changes. And those changes centered around where my treatments were to happen. I got approval to move to the brand-new treatment center that had opened the week between Christmas and the new year. I had already bonded with and had begun growing a relationship with that sweet nurse who had been there on that hard day when I learned "my" nurse was leaving. And she became my new "my nurse" when I transitioned over. My oncologist has an office there as well, so I was able to continue doing my office visits with him on the same day as treatment. It did mean adjusting to a new environment and moving to Thursdays for treatment and office visits versus Mondays as I'd done for six years. Another change to adjust to. But I felt like the timing of them had truly been orchestrated by God, so I felt peaceful about changes that I was able to choose for myself that came as a result of the changes that I didn't choose.

I started this chapter with the saying "the only thing you can count on is change." But when I did a Google search for scripture about change, Hebrews 13:8 came up: "Jesus Christ is the same yesterday and today and forever." And as I read it, peace washed over me, and I was reminded again to rest in this promise because "The Lord is trustworthy in all He promises and faithful in all He does" (Psalm 145:13b NIV). Enough said.

Control

> The Lord will keep your going out and your coming in from this time forth and forevermore.
>
> Psalm 121:8

> And we know that for those who love God all things work together for good for those who are called according to his purpose.
>
> Romans 8:28

Before I say anything else, I want to make it very clear that what I am about to share has absolutely nothing to do with my identity or my roles inside my home. I realize that, out of context, that makes no sense. But you will understand why I felt the need to start there very shortly.

I struggle. Often. By now, after reading this far, you know that already. However, one thing that I struggle with has its roots in my health situation, but it is not directly about cancer. It's about control. It's about choices. It's about identity. It's about feeling invisible. It's about feeling isolated.

Here's the deal: often I find it frustrating to feel that I have so little control over my own life because of cancer. I didn't choose to have cancer. No one does. But having metastatic breast cancer, knowing I will have cancer and cancer treatments for the rest of my life…that's a whole different monster. I don't get to choose my treatment schedule. It is dictated by medication protocol of how often I need to have the medications in order to keep my cancer in check. And the same with my scans. One of my medications necessitates an echocardiogram every three months to makes sure the medication isn't harming my heart. And even though that is very unlikely now, protocol, rules of the medicine dictate that I have that scan, or I won't be allowed to have the next treatment. And if I don't have the medication, my cancer wakes up and starts growing again. So I have an echo every three months. And the other scans? Well, the nature of the cancer I have is that it often mutates and comes back somewhere else in my body, resistant to the meds I'm on that keep my original caner asleep/stable/not growing. So every three months I have scans to make sure my original cancer is still stable and to check for indications that it has come back somewhere else. And every six months I have a brain MRI because that's one of the primary places that my kind of cancer frequently spreads to. Doing these things is not a choice. They are necessities. I have zero control over any of these things. If I want to keep fighting cancer, if I want to stay as healthy as possible for a cancer patient, these are the things that I must do, when I'm told to do them. As a result, it is virtually impossible for me not to see myself as a cancer patient. It dominates my thoughts and my action and my schedule. It invades every aspect of who I am and how I function. And very often it makes me feel invisible because the monster that I am fighting is invisible to everyone else. Because I'm not currently on chemo and am not bald, because I do not look like a "sick" person, those who don't know me and don't know my story have no clue when they see me that I actually am sick. That I actually am battling a monster. That I actually am a cancer patient.

Early on in my journey, this pattern of thinking was a constant companion. It was overwhelming and heavy and dark. But as I have settled more into this way of life, I don't struggle with it as often. Every now and again, however, it creeps back in. It's usually triggered by something else going on in my life. For instance, there was a brief period of time where there had been a lot going on in my family that was hard. Although it was health related, it wasn't about my health and really had nothing to do with me other than me needing to be available to take care of my grandson more than my typical schedule as his weekday caregiver while my daughter and son-n-law are at work. During this time period I was "on call" pretty much around the clock for several days in a row, and it was truly exhausting for me. At the time, my grandson was a little over two years old, and he was busy. Constant motion. So being his caregiver almost full time for several days in a row simply wore me out. You would think that when I finally got to bed at night during that time, I would have immediately fallen asleep. But because I frequently have trouble sleeping, there were several nights that I lay awake for hours, even though I was exhausted. Super frustrating. And as it often happens when I'm exhausted but am unable to sleep, lying in the darkness, my brain tends to go on autopilot into hard places. That's exactly what happened then. But this time, my brain carried me on a journey beyond cancer. I started thinking about other areas of my life where I feel I have no control or choice. Areas of my life where I feel like I've lost who I am and thus feel invisible. And it triggered a lot of thoughts and feelings that I didn't see coming.

Now, here's where I need to remind you of what I said at the start of this chapter. This is not about my role, who I am inside the walls of my home. I have no questions about who I am at home. I have no questions about the value of the roles I play in this part of my life. I am happy and secure here. But sometimes, in the darkness of a sleepless night, I think about life outside of these walls. The truth is, I don't have much of a "life" outside of my home now. I'm in a very different season now and I mostly love the things that season of my life has brought. I have the privilege and the joy of being the caregiver for all of my grandchildren while my children and children-in law work. And being able to do this is a direct answer to a prayer I prayed shortly after I was diagnosed. I asked God to let me live long enough to rock my grandbabies. And rock them I do! Five days a week I rock and care for my grandchildren. Talk about being blessed beyond measure! But there are parts of my life, BC (before cancer) that I miss. Some parts that I even mourn over the loss of. These are the things that I spent time thinking about during some of those sleepless nights. And the absence of these things, the absence of the people in my life that were associated with doing these things, often leave me feeling isolated.

I used to be a teacher. And I loved being a teacher. I mean LOVED being a teacher. And I miss it. I knew even when I was a little girl that I wanted to be a teacher. I went to college to prepare to be a teacher. It was my chosen profession. I knew who I was when I was a teacher. But you know what? I could never have been a teacher if I had not been chosen by someone to be a teacher. No amount of training or desire to be a teacher meant anything if I wasn't chosen by someone else to serve in that role. A principal, a preschool director, a group of parents seeking a teacher to homeschool their children during the pandemic, someone else was always in control, always had the decision-making power over my ability to be a teacher.

I used to be a children's choir coordinator/director. I LOVED leading children's choir ministry. I knew who I was when I served in that role. I felt confident in my abilities in that role. I felt like what I was doing was of eternal significance, and I felt honored and humbled and excited and fulfilled to be serving in that capacity. But initially I didn't seek that job out. Someone else chose me. Someone else came to me and said they wanted me to do that job. It was their decision to seek me out, their decision to offer me the opportunity, their decision to keep me in that role as long as I was at that church. And the decision to allow me to serve in that role in two other churches was also under someone else's control. A minister of music, a board of elders, they had decision making power over my ability to be a children's choir coordinator.

The truth is, every job I've ever had was because someone else chose to allow me to have that job. And as I thought about that, for a minute I was a little bitter. I thought, "Has everything about what I have done in my life, every way that I have identified myself been because of the control and choices of others?" The answer? Yep. Pretty much. And that made me mad! I did the work. I did the prep. I did the job. But someone else ultimately gets the credit, because it was their choice to allow me to do it? Well…kinda, yeah. And that led to the question "Is there really anything in my life that I have any control over?"

My thoughts were chaotic and coming at me faster than I could process. It went way beyond job-related stuff. Everything area of my life came into question. And every imaginable emotion came along with it. A little panic, a little sadness, a little anger, and ultimately a huge dose of relief and peace. I'm not sure I can really explain it all, But I'll try to give you just a glimpse of how I got there. See, many of the emotions I experiences were because my initial response to all of this chaos came from a very selfish place. MY lack of control. MY lack of choice. MY lack of understanding of who I am. So I felt panicked and angry and bitter and sad. But my next thought was a series of "why" questions. Most of the time, I despise "why" questions because they frequently have no answers. And that frustrates me. But on one particular night, as I lay in the darkness, wrestling with these thoughts, suddenly the struggle changed. This time was different. This time, the "why" questions took me to that place of relief and peace. Because the answer to each and every "why" question I thought of was "because God." I realize that this may seem counterintuitive considering I was struggling with the thought that someone else has always been in control of so many aspects of my life and how frustrated that made me feel. But submitting to God being in control of everything actually wasn't a hard concept for me at all. It was easy. It was a relief. It wasn't a new concept or even a new goal in my life. I've heard about this my whole life. I've always wanted to and tried to submit control of my life to God. I'm often pretty awful at it!

I fail at this way too often as is evident by how often I have to admit that I struggle with anger about feeling out of control in so many areas of my life. But this was different. Somehow, I felt differently about it. Somehow, I understood it differently. Somehow, I embraced it differently. Again, I'm not sure I can explain it, but I'm going to try.

It all comes down to this: I believe in a GOOD God. I believe He loves me and that no matter what happens in my life, no matter what He allows me to go through, He is still good, and He still loves me. I also believe that much of the hard that we all experience in life comes as a result of living in a fallen world, full of sin. And I believe that God can and does use all things, even the hard things, for His glory. He can and does use things that appear to be contrary to good FOR His good. He can and does use hard things in our lives for OUR good. I know it doesn't really make sense that I simultaneously believe that God doesn't control me like a puppet and yet I believe He is in control of all things in my life. But I do believe that. Here's how: God loves me y'all! He does! And I love Him with every fiber of my being. But. I mess up. A lot. Often. I struggle. A lot. Often. I try to take control of my own life. A lot. Often. And the results of those choices? A messy life full of fear and anger and bitterness and chaos and anxiety. And where does that get me? Nowhere. Literally. It gets me crying and wallowing in self-pity, and completely unable to accomplish anything productive or positive. And that is not where I want to be. I get there because I have wrapped my grubby little hands around my own life in an attempt to control it all by myself. But when I remember to open my hands and offer all the messiness up to God to repair and untangle and reorganize and get back on track and forgive, suddenly things make sense again, and the chaos turns to order, and the fear melts away. And then it happens. Peace. Sweet peace that only God can give me. It dawned on me that the peace comes from knowing that God IS in control. There's such relief in that, y'all! See, if God chooses something for my life, a job, a role, a place of service, then He is ultimately responsible for making sure that the task is accomplished. I may make a mess of it along the way. I may stumble in the process. I may even fail over and over before I reach the goal. But I believe that how hard or how easy the path to that goal is, how many times I stumble and mess up, all depends on how much I submit to God's control over the journey versus me trying to control it on my own. And I believe that if God has chosen it for me, then the task will be accomplished and the goal will be reached because He will do it through me. How can I NOT feel peace in that??? He loves me so much that if I will open my hands and give Him control over things, He will let me rest in the journey while He accomplishes His purpose in it. Yep, even in my cancer journey. I can rage against it every step of the way, or I can submit to His control in it and over it and have peace in the knowledge that He is bigger than cancer and that no matter what, He is still good.

I still struggle a bit with my identity. I'm no longer a teacher or a children's choir director. I'm not a receptionist or a music ministry associate. I'm not a salesperson or a tutor. I'm no longer any of the things I used to call myself, because I no longer do anything outside of my home now that has a label attached to it. So I still struggle sometimes with feeling like I don't know who I am anymore other than a cancer patient. And I still struggle with feeling isolated sometimes. I'll just have to keep working through all of that. And in the meantime, I will continue to take joy in being "Bibi" and taking care of my precious grandbabies. But I sure am happy to admit how good it feels to NOT be in control. I'm sure God will have to bring me back here over and over again as I stumble back into old habits of trying to control life on my own. But for now, I'm incredibly grateful for this peace.

Exile

> But seek the welfare of the city where I have sent you into exile, and pray to the Lord on its behalf, for in its welfare you will find your welfare.
>
> Jeremiah 29:7

It's funny to me when and where God chooses to speak to my heart. This particular day, He chose church. I know that sounds silly to be surprised that God spoke to my heart at church. I mean, of all places that He could choose to speak to us, church seems the most obvious one. But this was different. He spoke to me in church, during the sermon, directly from His Word. Except what He taught me had nothing to do with the sermon or the focal point of the passage of scripture as it related to the sermon topic. The sermon was a good one, and although I was fully engaged, was taking notes, and was learning, God pulled my eyes and my heart to two particular verses and used them to speak directly into my personal circumstances. There had some things that had been circling around in my head for a while. Things that I was dealing with that felt like playing tug o' war between my heart and my head. No. Tug o' war with God. The pull and push of what I felt like God was telling me to do versus what my head was telling me I am worthy of doing. But God used those Two verses from His Word to bring so many things that I had been struggling to make sense of into absolute clarity.

Before I go any further, let me give you some background context. Not long into the A.D. (after diagnosis) season of my life, I decided that since I was going to have to deal with cancer for the rest of my life, I wanted to find a way to do something positive with it. God opened the doors for me to do that initially through my cancer page on Facebook. I've already shared that I initially started the page to get information about my health to family and friends, eliminating the needs for multiple calls, texts, and emails. But I quickly realized that it also gave me a platform to share my story honestly. My whole story. The good, the bad, and the really ugly. It is a way for me to share what it's like to live day to day with metastatic cancer. But it was and is also my goal to be as transparent as possible about when I struggle with emotions like fear, sadness, and anger while, at the same time, sharing that these emotions exist in the same heart that truly, 100 percent believes that God loves me and cares for me in every detail of my life. I want people to understand that I believe that God is still good, in spite of the fact that He has chosen to allow me to walk this hard path. That I believe with my whole heart that God does not love me any less because I sometimes struggle. I want to share my story so that perhaps someone else who is in a similar same place will take heart that it is OK to not be OK and that God still loves them just like He still loves me.

Out of that Facebook page have come some other opportunities to share my story, and I have been amazed at how God has taken my circumstances and allowed me to use it to reach out to others who are walking in similar circumstances. It is my desire to use these opportunities to point others to the goodness of God and how precious His love is for us, even when we are at our most unlovable. But I struggle with a great deal of insecurity about this role. Not because of the story itself, but because I'm the one telling it. And I struggle with feeling unworthy. I know the whole me. The messy me. The sinner me. I know how often I fall short of being who Christ wants me to be. So who am I to share the goodness of God with anyone when I myself do often fail to exemplify Him? This feeling of unworthiness is not unique to me. So many of us struggle with feeling unworthy in one way or another. And although the world loves to spout "you are worthy" messages, truth is, none of us are worthy! None of us will ever be worthy. That's why we need Jesus!!! But there is another, more important truth: God doesn't wait until we are worthy to love us. And God doesn't call us to do things for Him because of anything worthy in us. It is His worthiness working through us. He uses our circumstances for His good. I know these truths. I believe these truths. And still, I've struggled with the idea that God wants to use unworthy me.

One of the ways that this has manifested itself is in my tendency to compare my story, my life to others' stories and lives. When I read posts on Facebook from other friends who are Christians dealing with cancer, I have let myself think that their stories are so much more faith filled. That they are so much better at pointing others to Christ. That they are on such a higher "Christian" plain than I am. And, again, I think about what a mess my life is. Past mistakes, daily mistakes, sin, ugliness, the very definition of being a "mess." And I think about how unworthy all of that makes me to say anything at all about my story. My messiness stacked against the faith-filled story of a friend…no comparison. And I can't help but feel that I should just stop and let the "good" Christians have the mic.

Another area that I've struggled with is in feeling isolated because of cancer. For one thing, no matter how hard you try, no matter how empathetic you want to be, unless you have walked this path, you just cannot understand. And I don't want you to have to understand. I don't desire this experience for anyone. I am grateful for all the support and words of encouragement and the empathy that people show me. It helps more that I can express. But at the end of the day, there are very few people in my life that really get what this is like. And even fewer of those that are in my daily life. None in my innermost circle. And that can be a very lonely place to live.

For another thing, it seems to me that people tend to have a pretty set idea of what breast cancer looks like:

1. Get diagnosed.
2. Have surgery to remove breasts.
3. Have treatment and lose hair.
4. Life goes on.
5. End of cancer story.

But that ain't it, y'all. That's not the whole story of a person diagnosed with breast cancer. And that certainly is not my story, because mine is a metastatic breast cancer story. I totally skipped over #2, and although life has gone on, cancer has continued to go with me. I will always have cancer. I will always have treatments. My cancer story will not end. I don't fit in with the pink ribbon crowd. Never will. My "crowd" is much less crowded, much less recognized by those outside the group, and even within the group, I think each of us feels pretty isolated. To the outside world, we look fine. I hear all the time from people that I haven't seen in a while, "But you look great!" And while a girl always loves hearing a compliment, what that feels like is "But you don't look sick." My friends, looking sick and being sick don't always go hand in hand. And when you are sick, but you don't look sick, if feels isolating.

Now that you have the backstory on all the things that had been swirling around in my head for months, let me tell you about another little incident that took all of this from my normal anxiety level to a whole new level. Some time ago I had a very heated discussion about something not even remotely related to cancer. A "how dare you" type comment was hurled at me because this person felt that I didn't have any business being involved in a particular situation because of some circumstances in my own life and was particularly hurtful. And I had a literal physical reaction. I was dizzy, and my blood pressure spiked. I was scared to drive myself home from where I was at the time, and my son had to come get me. I had to make him pull over once because I was sick to my stomach. It was frightening! At the time I blamed it all on that incident. Words are powerful, and these hurt me to my core. So it was easy to blame a fight and some careless words for the reaction I experienced. It was easier than facing that what was really happening was that those words spat at me in the middle of an argument were the out-loud manifestation of the thoughts inside my own head. My reaction to those words had little to do with the person who made it or the situation in which it was made. It had a great deal to do with all the tug o' war that was already going on in my head. All the messiness of my life. All the feelings of unworthiness. All the comparing I was doing. All of the things that Satan is so good at using to keep us in bondage to fear. There it all was, out in the open: I had no business telling my pitiful little story when I'm such a hot mess, and my story is of no use to anyone, least of all God. Someone else said it, so it must be real. And I was crippled by it. I spent a month being crippled by it. Until that particular Sunday.

The sermon was about how the church, our church specifically, is to be one with the city in which it is. How we, the church, are to impact the city. How we are to interact with and support and be among the people of our city. What the Bible says about it and what our pastor's desire is for our church in our city. He asked if our city would be impacted if suddenly our church ceased to exist. I found that question incredibly thought provoking and motivating. But while I was listening to the sermon, and I really was, God was planning something different in it for me personally, and it came directly from His Word. I believe that the phrase "God's Word is alive" means a lot of things. But for me, I believe that one way God's Word is alive is the way that He reveals to us what He wants us to learn from it based on our current circumstances and needs. He doesn't always reveal understanding of His Word in its entirety all at once. He reveals understanding as we are ready for it. As it speaks to specific circumstances in our lives. As our heart is prepared for it. For example, I may read something in the Bible that I've read many times before, but because of what my circumstance are at that moment, what my current needs are, God will open my eye to it in a new way and allow to me see or understand something new in it that directly applies to me. That particular Sunday was a version of that. The scripture that the pastor read from was 100 percent applicable to the sermon topic. But at the same time, it was 100 percent applicable to me personally, and it had absolutely nothing to do with the city I physically live in. The passage he used was Jeremiah 29, and two verses in particular spoke to me concerning my personal circumstances. The first is this: v. 4, "Thus says the Lord of hosts, the God of Israel, to all the exiles whom I have sent into exile from Jerusalem to Babylon." What stood out to me is "whom I have sent into exile." Often people who are going through a difficult time in their lives feel as if they are in exile. I, myself, often view having cancer as being in exile. Separated from the life I had dreamed for myself, but rather living a life that I could never have imagined. But that verse says, "whom I have sent into exile." Sometimes God intentionally sends us into exile. I had never given that much thought. Everything God does is intentional. So sometimes, sending us to a place of exile is intentional as well. Sometimes He allows us to go. But sometimes He sends us. Is it to teach us something? Is it to protect us from something? Is it for a time of waiting before He takes us into a new season? Only God can tell you the reasons He chooses. But I do believe that whatever the reason is that He chooses for sending us into exile, it is ultimately for our good. So that means that I also believe that God chose to allow me to live in the exile of cancer because He has something good that He wants to accomplish through it. And as much as I hate cancer, I can't help but see it as a blessing that God wants to do something good through me even if it's through cancer. I will never say that I believe that God gave me cancer. I don't believe that. I believe He allowed me to get cancer, and I believe that He chose to do something good because of it.

The second verse that spoke into my circumstances is this: v. 7, "But seek the welfare of the city where I have sent you into exile, and pray to the Lord on its behalf, for in its welfare you will find your welfare." Y'all! When I read that verse, it was like all of that stuff that had been spinning around in my head came together into a single, crystal-clear place all at once. Some of it was immediately apparent to me as I still sat in church. Some of it came together over the next few hours, and I reflected over the verse and as I thought back over the last months of my life. The immediate thought was this: my exile is cancer, but the city where God has sent me to live in exile is the people who walk similar paths. The people that God wants me to share my story with. My cancer community. And God wants me to pray for, invest in, support, and encourage my city by sharing my story in hopes that my story will encourage them. Sharing my story in my city for their welfare. And if I am obedient in doing what I feel that God is leading me to do, for the benefit of others, then my welfare is increased. BOOM!

So what about the other stuff? What do I do with all of that? Well, let's see...Feeling unworthy—already addressed that. I am. I always will be. But it's not about my worthiness. It's about the worthiness of God and His willingness to love me and use me in spite of my unworthiness.

Comparing my story to others' stories—God never intended my story to look just like someone else's. God has a plan and a purpose that He is carrying out through each person's story. He hasn't asked me to tell anyone else's personal story. He will call and lead them to carry out His plan for their stories. All He asked me to do is tell my story. Tell my city the truth about what my cancer journey looks like. The truth about the times that I struggle. The truth about when it is hard for me. The truth about the fact that I'm a hot mess. But that even when all of the struggle and hard and mess is happening, God doesn't love me any less. God is still good. And I am no less saved. I am His child, loved by Him, watched over by Him just as much on the days when I'm a hot mess as I am on the days that I am strong and courageous. God wants someone to hear that so that they know that sometimes it's OK to not be OK and that God is still good in the midst of the hard and the scary and the painful.

Who am I to share anything when my life is so messy? God didn't ask me to share about how to clean up all your messes. God didn't ask me to tell you how you were supposed to do anything. God didn't ask me to tell you what you're supposed to do or what you're not supposed to do. God didn't ask me to be a perfect example of anything to anyone. God doesn't expect me to be perfect before he's capable of using my story. I don't need to have all of my stuff figured out for my story to be impactful to someone else. God simply asked me to share my story honestly. So that's what I'm going to try to keep doing.

I know there will always be times when anxiety and insecurity creep in. Satan is good at getting us frail humans to fall prey to insecurity. And in doing so, we sometimes fail to do what God has called us to do. And that's Satan's plan. To keep the goodness of God from being shared. So I know that I will have to work hard to battle against that. But now these verses are in my arsenal, and I can use them whenever I need them, because God's Word is sharper than any sword and is forever true. And in the meantime, I will keep sharing my story whenever God opens up the opportunity to do so. And I will continue to seek opportunities to help others in their cancer journeys. That's the entire purpose in writing this book.

Not the End

> For I know the plans I have for you, declares the Lord, plans for welfare and not for evil, to give you a future and a hope. Then you will call upon me and come and pray to me, and I will hear you. You will seek me and find me, when you seek me with all your heart. I will be found by you, declares the Lord, and I will restore your fortunes and gather you from all the nations and all the places where I have driven you, declares the Lord, and I will bring you back to the place from which I sent you into exile.
>
> Jeremiah 29:11–14

I've struggled with how to write an ending to this book. And in a conversation with my daughter about it, she said, "Maybe you're struggling with how to end the book because your cancer story isn't over." She was exactly right. That precisely explained how I felt without me even realizing it. In my mind, all stories are supposed to have a neat ending, all the details wrapped up in a pretty bow, nothing left hanging, no unanswered questions. But that's not where my story is. And I'm grateful for that. I am hoping, instead, that my story is at best in the middle and that there is much more still to come.

But this isn't really a storybook, is it? So what exactly is it, and how do I bring it to a close? Well, it's simply my written hope that something about what I have learned thus far about living with cancer will help someone else. My hope is that I can encourage someone else to believe with their whole heart that no matter what God allows us to go through, no matter what path He leads us on, He loves us and is good. So I decided to close by making a list of the things I share with each person that God brings into my life that is facing their own journey with a cancer diagnosis. A couple of these I have already touched on earlier in this book. But here it all is in a short, concise list. I hope this will be helpful to you or someone you love.

1. Stay off the internet. I already shared this in an earlier chapter, but I feel strongly enough about it that I feel it bears repeating. There is so much information about cancer out there that is inaccurate or out of date or that can be unnecessarily scary. So get your information from your doctor. If you do want to go on the internet, ask your doctor what

sites are reliable and up to date, and stick to those. As for me, I try to stay away from online cancer sites altogether.

2. Many people are going to throw cancer stories and cancer advice at you. Please keep in mind that they are typically well-meaning, but they often say things that are insensitive and unhelpful. Particularly the stories about everyone they know who has died from cancer. I'll never understand why people feel compelled to share those stories, but for some reason, they just can't help themselves. Give them grace, pretend to listen politely, and let it go in one ear and out the other.

3. Start a list on your phone labeled "Ask My Doctor." When questions come to your mind that you want to ask at your next appointment, write them on that list immediately. Cancer and life in general can be overwhelming and hectic, and we forget things that we meant to ask. Things that could be important. So write them down.

4. The beginning of a cancer diagnosis is information overload! So much will be thrown at you, and it's almost impossible to retain and process it all at once. Ask your doctor if you can record your appointments/discussions with him/her so that you can listen back over them later to refresh

your memory. It is also extremely helpful to take someone with you to these appointments, especially early on, who can be an extra set of ears for you as you are learning more about your diagnosis and your treatment plan.

5. Your emotions will likely be all over the place. Hopeful one minute and scared the next. And that's OK! Allow yourself the space and time and grace to feel it all. And if you feel like lying on the bed and crying your eyes out or standing in the yard and screaming at the heavens, then do it! Get those emotions out however you need to. It's OK to curl into a tight ball and hide from the world. For a little while. Just don't stay there. Don't stay in the fear and the frustrated and the dark and the anger. Feel it. Own it. Wallow in it even. And then get up and face it again with the confidence that God is right in the middle of it with you and will carry you through it all. He is in control, and HE WILL NEVER LEAVE YOU!

6. Give yourself grace when you are struggling. Be honest with yourself and with God about it. He already knows anyway. He gave us all those emotions. He knows we deal with them all. Be honest with Him when you're struggling, when you have questions, when you're angry, when you're scared, with all of it! And have peace that through all of it,

even when your faith feels small, you are no less loved by God in those moments than in the moments when your faith is at its strongest.

7. God is still good! So even on the hardest days, rest in His love for you and in His never-failing goodness.

Thank you for choosing to be a part of my journey. Thank you for being with me in my exile. Thank you for being my city. I pray for your welfare and that in it, I will find my own. And I rejoice that one day the Lord will bring me out of exile and into His glorious presence forever.

> ...yet I will rejoice in the Lord; I will take joy in the God of my salvation.
>
> Habakkuk 3:18b

www.ingramcontent.com/pod-product-compliance
Lightning Source LLC
LaVergne TN
LVHW041711060526
838201LV00043B/682